A SENSE OF BELONGING

A SENSE OF BELONGING

From Castro's Cuba to the U.S. Senate,
One Man's Pursuit of the American Dream

Senator Mel Martinez

with Ed Breslin

THREE RIVERS PRESS
NEW YORK

Library of Congress Cataloging-in-Publication Data
Martinez, Mel (Melquiades Rafael), 1946–
A sense of belonging: from Castro's Cuba to the U.S. Senate, one man's pursuit
of the American dream / Mel Martinez ; with Ed Breslin.
1. Martinez, Mel (Melquiades Rafael), 1946–   2. Legislators—United States—
Biography.   3. United States. Congress. Senate—Biography.   4. Republican National
Committee (U.S.)—Biography.   5. United States. Dept. of Housing and Urban
Development—Officials and employees—Biography.   6. Politicians—Florida—
Biography.   7. Cuban Americans—Biography.   8. Immigrants—United States—
Biography.   9. Cuba—History—1933–1959—Biography.   I. Breslin, Ed.   II. Title.
E901.1.M37A3 2008
328.73092—dc22
[B]   2008014963

ISBN 978-0-307-40541-8

Printed in the United States of America

Design by Leonard Henderson

10 9 8 7 6 5 4 3 2 1

First Paperback Edition

Man loves liberty, even if he does not know that he loves it. He is driven by it and flees from where it does not exist.

—José Marti

Dictators ride to and fro upon tigers which they dare not dismount. And the tigers are getting hungry.

—Winston Churchill

CONTENTS

FAREWELL: The last photo of my family together in
Cuba. *From left to right:* My brother, Ralph *(in front);*
me *(behind);* my father; my sister, Margarita
(in my dad's arms); my mother.

DEPARTURES AND ARRIVALS

SOME DAYS ARE MIRACULOUS. You feel the grace of God at work in the universe as surely as you feel, in your exhilaration, your own heartbeat.

As I stood at the back of the United States Senate chamber on a cold January morning, I felt a dash of nerves, a rush of joy, and a wealth of gratitude. In a few moments I would be summoned forward to take the oath of office as senator from the state of Florida.

My anticipation only grew as I watched other newly elected senators make their way down the aisle. When my turn finally arrived I swallowed hard and started toward the presiding table, keenly aware that I was about to swear an oath that U.S. senators had been taking for more than two centuries. As soon as I entered the well of the Senate chamber I looked up and spotted my family seated above in the gallery, peering over the railing, smiling down at me. Seeing them warmed and relaxed me. There sat my wife, Kitty, and our three children, Lauren, John, and Andrew. I spied my younger brother, Ralph, and I immediately thought of our father, since their gestures and facial expressions were so similar. Our dad had passed away nearly a decade earlier, but seeing Ralph, I was reminded that he was there with us nonetheless.

When I made eye contact with my mother I got a big lump in my throat. Still healthy in her eighties, my mom, Gladys Ruiz Martinez, was beaming. She popped up and blew me a kiss, a look of pure joy on her face. We did not need to speak; everything made sense as we connected and communicated, one spirit to another. It was not simply my mother's pride that moved me. Seeing her face transported me to a moment forty-three years earlier when she and I had likewise locked eyes. But the look on her face back then was not one of joy but of pure agony.

On the afternoon of February 6, 1962, at the age of fifteen, I was separated from my mother—in fact, from my entire family and from everything else I knew. That day I boarded a Pan Am DC-6 that took me away from my native Cuba to the United States, a land where I knew virtually no one and whose language I did not speak. Leaving Cuba was a wrenching decision, but one that my family and I had determined to be my only option once Communist dictator Fidel Castro and his totalitarian regime seized power. Though just a teenager, I had to escape this dictator's government at once, and the only way I could get out would be on my own, on this flight to a foreign land. Before I boarded the plane I was held for hours in the Havana airport's *pecera* ("fishbowl"), the glass-enclosed space where passengers leaving the country waited to be interrogated (and in some cases even strip-searched) by Castro's olive-clad men. My mother stood on the other side of the *pecera*'s glass, unable to speak to me or to touch me. We could not be certain when, or even if, we would see each other again, and the torment was etched on her face. Her desperate expression was the last thing I saw before I left my homeland.

This is why taking the oath of office as a United States senator was much more than merely the highlight of my political career: it marked the culmination of a journey, of a long and exceedingly unlikely odyssey from a small town in Cuba to a senatorial posting on Capitol Hill. Those two moments with my mother—her look of anguish, then of ecstasy—represent the dominant markers along this path. Both are imprinted on my memory; I cannot see one without seeing the other.

My journey has taught me that it is not an empty cliché that this country is a land where dreams can and do come true. It is also true, I have learned, that even in the face of painful experiences we must remember and emphasize the positive. I have endured political turmoil, the constant fear that comes with life under a totalitarian regime, the wrenching experience of exile from one's native country, and the loneliness and isolation of living in a new land. Despite all that, I have been blessed with extraordinary good fortune: I escaped Castro's Cuba even though a foolish mistake on my part nearly sabotaged my parents' painstaking plans for my getaway. I left for America just months before Castro slammed the door on the refugee programs that had allowed me to escape. I slowly developed a sense of belonging in my adopted home of America. And ultimately, after a long and unbearable separation, I was reunited with the family I left behind at the Havana airport that day in 1962.

America is my home now, and I will forever feel grateful to have enjoyed its freedoms when so many from my native country have been trapped under Cuba's Communist regime. My prayer is that the Cuban people will one day soon enjoy freedom of their own.

To this day I have not set foot in Cuba since my plane took off from Havana on a February afternoon in 1962. But even now, all these decades later, it remains my deepest wish to show Kitty and our children the land where I was born, to be able to walk in a free Cuba. I will never forget my homeland.

LIFE AT THE BEACH: Me and Pancho, the pet goat
that my father, a veterinarian, kept at our little
beach house in Playa Uvero.

Chapter 1

HOMELAND

DARKNESS. A PORCH. A warm ocean breeze. The sound of voices—my father's, and those of the old fishermen gathered around him. Stories about fishing, storms, boats, life. These are my earliest memories. They are memories collected at my family's quaint summer beach house at Playa Uvero, fifteen miles from our hometown of Sagua la Grande. My father's father had built the house in this fishing village on the northern coast of Cuba long before it became a popular summer vacation spot. At that time Playa Uvero was the year-round home only to charcoal makers and professional fishermen. When my grandfather and other early vacationers settled, they built their houses near the locals' homes, far back from the water's edge. Later vacationers built houses on stilts close to the shore.

Sadly, I never knew my grandfather—he died when I was only forty days old—but the beach house he put up in the 1920s is the backdrop for some of my most vivid recollections of childhood. That porch in particular: it's as if I can still hear the buzzing of insects in my ear and see the weathered fishermen trading stories with my father.

My father, who had been coming to this village every summer since his own childhood, was very outgoing and friendly and loved to talk. He had a booming voice that, along with his heavyset frame, made him a real presence. So our porch became a social center, with men from the village gathering there most nights. I would plop down in my dad's lap or, later as I grew bigger, would sit cross-legged on the porch, listening to them talk. We would be enshrouded in darkness, for the simple reason that our rustic little home had no electricity. A small windmill supplied only enough electricity to charge a car battery, which in turn powered a couple of lightbulbs. We wouldn't have used the bulbs on the porch, since the darkness helped keep away the ever-present bugs. For additional lighting when needed, we used kerosene lanterns.

The stories these men shared were mesmerizing to a young boy. The old fishermen had lived through World War II, when German submarines combed the waters off Cuba. One man from the village told a story about picking up some German sailors who were adrift on a raft, hauling them into his fishing boat, bringing them ashore, and turning them over to the authorities. It amazed me that submariners from across the ocean had apparently patrolled so close to our little home.

My father was a veterinarian in Sagua. Just as his father had done before him, he would commute on weekdays in the summer, taking a small railcar to and from Sagua, about an hour's ride through the green sugarcane fields of Central Resulta, the sugar mill in Sagua la Grande. Meanwhile, the rest of our family stayed in Playa Uvero from mid-June to mid-August. I didn't mind the simple living conditions—the lack of electricity and running water, the cistern we relied on, the charcoal-burning stove and the kerosene single-burner stove we had. I enjoyed the novelty of taking a shower at Uvero. The bathroom shower was nothing more than a five-gallon tank with a showerhead welded to the bottom. We would fill the tank with warm water and hoist it using a pulley attached to the ceiling. There was a cleat on the wall where we would tie off the line holding it up. Once it was secure, the bather released the water by pulling a cord one way for "on" and the other way for "off." Simple, but ingenious.

I loved spending the summers at Playa Uvero with my mother and my younger brother, Ralph. There were always aunts, uncles, and cousins visiting as well. Every Sunday, my great-uncle Mariano would come for the big seafood lunch we shared as a family and would bring fresh bread from Sagua with him. Sunday lunches were always on the front porch, with the breeze gently blowing.

Playa Uvero was an idyllic setting for a boy. Cuba was a kind of paradise to me, unrivaled in its physical beauty, its climate, and the warmth and friendliness of its people. I got to see the sun sparkle on the water in the daytime and then watch it set as a fiery red ball at dinnertime. As a small child I played for hours in the sand, and as I got older I would pass entire days swimming and fishing.

My father passed many things on to me—not least being my name, Melquiades, which was also the name of my grandfather and my great-grandfather before him. A love of fishing was one of the many traits I shared with my dad. He was big on fishing, and he taught me the techniques of hand-line fishing and net fishing. We just threw the line out with a weight on it and held it firmly in hand, then pulled when a fish struck. We also would cast a net for bait, snaring small fish in the mesh. When I got older I got my own small cast net. I developed a routine: catch bait with my cast net, then go fish until lunchtime.

My dad would often go out in our twenty-three-foot boat and fish for the whole weekend. Sundays would be filled with anticipation for his return. My mother would bring my brother and me to the shore in the afternoon to await his arrival. Often when Papi came back, his boat would be practically overflowing with fish—grouper, snapper, yellowtail. It was more than we could ever eat in those days before reliable refrigeration. So he would wait for the commercial fishermen (many of them his old friends) to come in and sell their catch on the beach. Once he was sure he wasn't undercutting any of the professionals, he would give away his extra fish.

When I was around ten, my dad finally started taking me on overnight trips. Sleeping and eating on the boat seemed like heaven on earth. On one occasion Papi bought lobsters from some commercial fishermen. The lobsters he cooked made for not only a wonderful dinner but also a rare breakfast treat: the next morning I ate the leftover lobster cold with stale Cuban bread.

When I turned twelve I received the greatest summer gift ever. My parents surprised me with my own twelve-foot rowing dinghy, complete with a live well. This was a dream come true. It was handy for my father's fishing trips—my job was to row while he and the other adults threw a cast net for bait fish—but during the week, it was all mine. I would row out to my favorite fishing spots with a friend. Being out there in the sea on my own gave me a quiet sense of independence.

Fishing left me with memories of the best of Cuba and the best of my childhood. To this day when asked I will always answer that it is the thing I miss the most about Cuba.

❖   ❖   ❖

SO MANY OF my recollections of Cuba involve family. The whole family gathered every summer at Playa Uvero, of course, but that was not the only place. It wasn't unusual in Cuban families to have several generations living under one roof. That was the situation I experienced for the first six years of my life. We lived with my

FAMILY: My brother, Ralph, and I with my grandmother Graciela and our cousins. I am at the left, while Ralph is on the right.

father's mother—my grandmother Graciela. Her home was a large upstairs apartment located right in the center of Sagua la Grande. Grandmother Graciela had a pretty balcony in the front and a little courtyard in the back, where I have faint memories of riding my tricycle and my scooter. I also recall going downstairs beneath the balcony and getting the bus to take me to first grade and my first school experience. My father drilled into me that when I got on the bus I was to say good morning to the bus driver.

My own little universe was all right there in Sagua la Grande, a city of maybe thirty thousand people located on the banks of the Sagua River, about two hundred and twenty miles east of Havana, due south of Miami. When I got a little older I could go everywhere in town on my bike—my school, the ball field, my grandmother's house, my uncle's house.

Sagua, though not a big city, was an important commercial center, with a sugar mill, a foundry that made parts for sugar mills throughout the country, and a thriving shipping business out of the Port of Isabela de Sagua. The surrounding agricultural area was rich in sugarcane, rice, and cattle. But those aspects of Sagua did not really enter my world. It was simply a great place to grow up.

Only about twelve miles from Sagua was the tiny rural town of Quemado de Güines, home to my mother's mother, Pilar Caro Ruiz. My mother loved going home to see her mother. When Ralph and I were young, she would often take us there for weekend visits. I would sleep in that little wooden house and wake up with the sun streaming in and the clip-clop of horses going down the street. An old milkman would deliver on horseback, perched in the saddle with a couple of big milk jugs strapped on either side of the horse in straw bags. He would sing out to the ladies to come out of the house. They would bring a container and he would pour the milk into it. That was one of those little things I vividly recall—pastoral, rural, rustic. It was typical of the life of a small Cuban town in the 1950s. This was a long way from the glittering lights of Havana's nightlife.

❖ ❖ ❖

ADVENTURES WERE NEVER hard to find, even when we were not at the beach. My grandfather Melquiades, who built the beach house, also owned a small soda-bottling factory in Sagua, Compañía de Refrescos Purita, S.A. After his death, my great-uncle Mariano and my father ran the business with their partners. Since my dad was busy with his veterinarian job, Mariano oversaw the day-to-day operations. I was constantly in and out of that little factory. Going there was great fun for me. Many of the men who worked at the plant watched me grow up. When I was a little boy, the bookkeeper entertained me in the office. Later, as I grew older, I did some real work with the men. Sometimes I'd help load the trucks with cases of soda and then ride shotgun for the deliveries at restaurants and bars in and around Sagua. Other times I'd load bottles into the bottle-washing machine. Little bits here and there to help with the family business.

Aside from the free sodas and the camaraderie with the guys, I loved spending time with Uncle Mariano. He never married and had no children, so as the oldest grand-nephew, I was his favorite. He was grumpy and demanding to the men who worked at the plant but always had a softer side for me. Like the beach house, the soda factory was a favorite place of mine.

So too was my uncle Rinaldo's dairy farm. The farm was slightly outside Sagua la Grande, and it was very beautiful, with flat green pastures. I spent a lot of happy days at my uncle's farm. I was fortunate to have a horse I could ride there. I'd walk my horse under a guava tree and fill the saddlebags with guavas to snack on and bring home to our family.

But even better was spending time with Uncle Rinaldo. He and his wife, my mother's sister Yolanda, had no children at the time, so I was the beneficiary of his unfulfilled paternal instincts. On days I didn't have school, Rinaldo would pick me up in the afternoons and bring me along to "help" with the chores. I don't think I was much help, but I loved saddling up our horses and riding all afternoon, checking fences or moving cattle from one pasture to another, and then at the end of the day unsaddling the horses, watering them, and putting them out in their pasture next to the barn.

For a boy this was sheer pleasure, but I also got to see the back-breaking work my uncle and his helpers put in to keep the farm running. Often they would put the cattle and other livestock through vats to delouse them and rid them of ticks. I learned to milk cows, to round up animals, to take care of the horses, and to manage the calves, which were smaller and more manageable for a boy. Of course, for me this was an afternoon's entertainment, but for them all this work came after having awoken hours before sunrise.

Both the soda factory and the farm were, like the small beach house, the scene of vivid memories of my youth in Cuba. Within just a few years, though, both places would be gone—two more casualties of the radical "revolution" that was soon to sweep my homeland.

❖   ❖   ❖

AS A VETERINARIAN, my father was familiar with the animal issues Uncle Rinaldo and other farmers faced. He dealt with all kinds of animals, but focused mostly on cattle, horses, and pigs on the farms outside Sagua. Just as I helped out on my uncle's farm, I would tag along with my dad as he made his rounds; as I got older, I would also help him out by carrying his bag, holding animals for him so he could give them shots, and carrying medications for him. He would wear a white doctor's coat with his name stitched on his left pocket. That left pocket always carried his Parker fountain pen.

As a veterinarian in a country setting, he had a range of responsibilities. Much of the time he headed out to the country to tend to farm animals. One time a horse encephalitis epidemic broke out and he was incredibly busy. Everybody had to have their horses vaccinated for fear they would lose them. Sometimes, too, he had to inspect the slaughterhouse, which was certainly an eye-opening experience for a kid. It was smelly, bloody, and noisy, and we were never there long. But we went often enough that I got to see a member of the Guardia Rural (Rural Guard), an official who came on horseback to check on the slaughterhouse, wearing what would be known in the States as a Smokey the Bear hat.

I loved making the rounds with my father, bumping along dusty dirt roads in a 1950 Chevrolet with a scoop back. That old Chevy sedan was his car for business—no pickup, no panel truck, no jeep. My dad hated to drive the stick shift. Sometimes he would get stuck and we'd have to jump out and rock that old car to get it going again. This made for high adventure—in mud sometimes a foot deep. If we tried to take a shortcut and we ended up stuck on a country road, he was always ready with an old Spanish saying like *"Nunca dejes camino por vereda,"* which means "Never leave the main road for the trail."

Many times, obviously, my father would need to care for sick animals, but sometimes the job was delivering a calf. He would always get to bickering with the farmer for not having called him sooner. Farmers were trying to avoid the vet fee, of course. But by trying to deliver the calf themselves they made the job more difficult for my dad. So he would fuss with them, saying, "Why are you calling me now? You should have called me yesterday." My father, though, was not one to argue long, especially when there was business to attend to. He'd quickly take care of the problem.

Then, whether we were visiting a nice big house in the country or the most humble little dirt-floored, thatch-roofed *bohío,* we would always be invited in for coffee. The families took pride in hosting us for *café.* And my father, big talker that he was, was glad to sit and chat. He loved to hunt, so often he'd ask about deer in the area to scout for deer-hunting season. He always introduced me as *"el heredero"* (the heir), which I suppose was some old Cuban way of referring to your oldest son, but mainly I sat there and soaked it all in, just as I did those many nights on the porch at the beach.

My dad had friends everywhere he went. If farmers could pay him, they paid him; if not, they would give him a chicken and some eggs. He said he charged them what they could afford. If they were substantial ranchers who owned imported cattle from the United States, he would charge them a fair price. But if the client was some poor guy for whom that one little cow and calf were his only liveli-hood, my dad would let him pay what he could. Throughout my childhood people would show up at our door with a big box of man-goes or a couple of chickens. That was their way of paying him back. They took care of the vet, and he took care of them. Years later, one of his clients, Carlos Manuel Garcia, would tell me, "Your father was a great vet and a great man, but his fault was he didn't know what to charge for his work." Carlos told me of having to pursue my father to get a bill and then, when he finally got it, finding that it was surely too low—so he overpaid. Charging for his work was the hard-est thing for my dad.

While my father was a bit of a soft touch, he took a great deal of pride in the work he did, and was dedicated to veterinary medicine. He had attended veterinary school at the University of Havana, the first in his family to go to college. While there, he and two other students formed a close friendship and always studied together. They were proud to finish as the best three in their class; they stayed close through the years after graduation. I don't think my dad had been a great student until he got to the university, but he truly loved being a vet. People who knew him when he was young would tell me, "I knew your dad was going to be a vet. He loved animals and always had pets when he was a kid." His vocation and avocation were the same.

Long after he had left the University of Havana, my dad worked hard at staying on the cutting edge, learning the latest techniques, treatments, and innovations in veterinary medicine. He kept up with his profession by reading the scientific newsletters and journals, including some written in English, a language he didn't speak well. He also did his own laboratory work, in a room in my grandmother's house set aside as his office and makeshift lab, complete with microscope, slides, and other equipment. Oftentimes I would go with him when he drew blood all day from a whole herd of cattle. Then he would work long hours at night doing the tests on all the blood he'd drawn. He couldn't send the blood samples and slides "over to the lab." He *was* the lab. This was the life of a country vet back then in Cuba.

I learned a lot from my father about being a professional and taking pride in the work you do. He frequently said one learned the basic skills in school but only became a veterinarian out in the field. How right he was about the importance of experience and the commitment to performing well. I picked up so much from my father, and as a parent I hope I have passed at least some of it on. When you have had a great father you wonder if you have lived up to the standard that he set.

❖   ❖   ❖

THERE IS THE perception that the Cuban exiles who fled to the United States in the 1960s were all wealthy. That's not true. My family was comfortable but not rich. My great-uncle Mariano, the one who managed the soda factory, would help my family financially. At the end of every summer, as the new school year approached, he'd say to my dad, "When you get ready to buy the schoolbooks, let me know because I want to pay for them." My parents were grateful to Mariano for that. Remember, my dad didn't bill for his work half the time.

My mother's upbringing had been anything but luxurious. She came from modest beginnings in that house in the little town of Quemado de Güines. She was the fourth of six children—four girls and two boys. In her teens she quit high school to help the family make ends meet. She moved to Sagua la Grande to live with her older sister Ondina, and eventually moved into the home of the Huergos, a family that owned a hair salon. This is where she learned to be a hairdresser. Her father died when she was only eighteen, and her earnings became even more crucial to her family then.

My mother kept working even after she married my father and they had moved into my grandmother Graciela's apartment. She set up a tiny beauty parlor right there in Graciela's home, in a back room. It became a sort of social club. The ladies would come, sit and have coffee with my grandmother, and then have their hair done. But the work remained an important source of extra income for our family. And the skills my mother developed as a hairdresser would prove vital when my parents came to America.

After living for several years in my grandmother's apartment, my parents had saved enough to build a home of their own. Our family was expanding: Ralph was born in 1950, four years after I was. So around 1952, my dad sold a little farm he owned to come up with the money to buy property bordering farm country outside

MAMI: My mother and I, in the early days
when we lived with Graciela.

Sagua. The house would be located in the area called Reparto de Oña, which was on the route to Sagua's sugar mill, Central Resulta.

Like most things with the Martinezes, this building project was a family affair. The architect who designed the house was my uncle Mario Esquiroz, the husband of my father's older sister Luisa, who lived and worked in Havana. My father's younger brother, my uncle Eduardo, was also an architect. Unlike Uncle Mario, Eduardo lived in town, so he oversaw the construction.

When the house was finished we were thrilled to live in it. It was not grandiose by any stretch of the imagination—just a three-bedroom, two-bath house—but it was ours. I loved the new yard we could play in. The neighborhood was great for me because there were enough kids to form teams for pickup baseball and other games. Baseball especially became a fixation of mine, something I played throughout my youth.

By 1955 our modern new house even got a TV, black-and-white with rabbit ears. That allowed me to watch the World Series, Yankees versus Dodgers. Although the games were played in New York, the ones we saw were broadcast with a Spanish commentator. This was a breakthrough, technologically. The Cuban television stations would send up an airplane to pick up the signal out of Miami and retransmit it into Cuba—a little bit like TV Martí does now in order to penetrate Castro's embargo on information. For a baseball fan like me, getting to see the World Series was a treat. The only problem was that on weekdays I had to go back to school for the afternoon session.

In Cuba we went to school from 8 A.M. until noon, then went home for lunch. The World Series would start about 1 P.M., and I would get to watch the top of the first inning, but then we had to head back to school by 1:30. By the time we got out of class, at 4:30, the game would be over. As soon as classes got out we'd run over to the food vendor across the street from school to find out the final score.

In Game 7 of the 1955 World Series, when I was just shy of my ninth birthday, the big news was that one of Cuba's native sons was the difference maker. Edmundo "Sandy" Amoros went into left field for the Dodgers as a late-inning defensive replacement that day. Almost immediately Yankee slugger Yogi Berra hit a line drive near the left field foul line. Amoros came out of nowhere to make an extraordinary catch, reaching out to snag the ball in the corner and then finishing an amazing double play by throwing out Gil McDougald at first base. It was one of the most famous catches in baseball history, and it sealed the Brooklyn Dodgers' first World Series victory. To us Cubans, who watched Amoros play for the famous Almendares Club in the Cuban winter league, this was a proud day.

I didn't get to see Amoros's catch live, but the next year I watched Don Larsen get revenge for the Yankees when he pitched a perfect game against the Dodgers. I wasn't in school that day and stayed glued to the TV set the whole game. I can still see Yogi Berra charging the mound and jumping on Larsen to celebrate.

When I got older, my friends and I had to go to much greater lengths to watch the World Series. The problem was that after Castro took over, he cut out the World Series transmissions into Cuba. So we would take turns going up to the roof to redirect the antenna, trying to pick up transmissions from Miami stations. What we were able to get was snowy at best.

❖   ❖   ❖

SCHOOL MAY HAVE kept me from the World Series at times, but I loved it. The elementary school, a Catholic institution called Sagrado

Corazón de Jesús, was a huge part of my life in Cuba. It was more than just a place to learn. In going there I was following in my dad's footsteps, since he had attended the school as well. Steeped in tradition, the boys' school was housed in a magnificent old building erected in the early part of the twentieth century. The big courtyard in the center featured a fountain topped by a statue of Jesus the teacher. The school was part of the Jesuit educational tradition in Cuba until about 1957, when an order of priests and brothers of the Misioneros Sagrados Corazones took charge of our education.

The school chapel, with its soaring steeple, was a central part of life at Sagrado Corazón de Jesús. We went to mass every morning. As an altar boy I served mass many times, saying the responses in Latin, as was required in those pre–Vatican II days. Learning those responses was the extent of my education in Latin, actually, since the principal foreign language taught to us as part of the curriculum was English. But I must say, we didn't learn much English in grade school. I'd have to learn the language on my own, later.

The Catholic-school environment developed my strong Catholic faith from a very early age. That faith was to be a source of strength throughout my life. Sagrado Corazón de Jesús was also responsible for strengthening my father's faith. For many years it was my mother who took Ralph and me to mass; my dad did not regularly attend. But over the years he formed a strong friendship with the priest who became my most important mentor at the school, Father Gayá, who taught history and was the rector. Father Gayá was originally from Majorca, a Spanish island in the Mediterranean. He worked with my father to the point that he brought him back to the practice of his faith. I can remember the joy in our home that Papi would now be coming to church with us regularly on Sundays. This is just one of the many reasons I felt such a debt of gratitude to this wise priest.

Much more than an educational facility and a religious institution, school was a social hub and a recreational center as well. More and more, the games I had started playing in the neighborhood migrated over to the school grounds. We played ball all the time at school. Sometimes we played soccer, and we certainly played more often than the typical Cuban kid ever would have. That is because so many of our teachers were Spanish priests who had fallen under the game's influence as boys back in Spain. But baseball and basketball were much more common. Baseball, especially, was huge. It was *the* sport in Cuba. Baseball was king.

The games at school carried over to weekends. We'd head over to school on Saturdays, and the priests would let us in and give us the equipment. We would play baseball and basketball pickup games that lasted the entire day. We would play until dark, hours on end. It was the lost art of boys playing ball because they loved it. We didn't need a coach or a dad, expensive equipment or a manicured field. We didn't even require an umpire. We simply went at it, playing hard, officiating among ourselves, sometimes arguing a call.

The games got more organized when the school sponsored a Little League team. I was ten or eleven when these games started. Little League—or Cubanitos—marked the first time I played when everyone had uniforms.

Baseball and, to a slightly lesser extent, basketball became my passions. Really, these games were my reason for living as a boy. And I became good at them. My dad, who came to some of my Little League games when his work schedule allowed, had played ball in his youth, so maybe I inherited some of his athletic ability. Papi had been a first baseman when he played as a boy, but I played mostly catcher. Well, at least until I had a collision at home plate and had to have several stitches on my forehead. The next day I was playing third base, in order not to tear the stitches out with the catcher's mask.

But I just kept playing the games, I loved them so much. Little did I know then that sports would be a calling card for me when I came to America.

❖ ❖ ❖

AROUND THE SAME time I started Little League, I joined the Boy Scouts. I was one of the first to join the Scouts when they started in Sagua. For the next three years I threw myself into Scouting. I especially enjoyed the overnight camping trips we took. We didn't have state parks in my part of Cuba, so camping meant hiking to the woods on someone's farm. In those days we had big, heavy, inflexible cotton tents, nothing like the compact, light ones campers use now. I didn't mind, though; I got a lot out of our camping adventures—learning to survive in the wilderness, to manage with just the bare essentials. It was like the summers at my family's primitive house by the beach: sometimes by cutting out the normal distractions of life we could enjoy ourselves even more. Scouting taught me some practical skills—I still remember how to tie the knots they taught us, as I've used them for outdoor adventures as an adult—but more important, it gave me self-confidence and taught me something about leadership.

The Boy Scouts were another key element of a happy childhood. After all, how much did I really have to complain about, playing ball at school, fishing and swimming at the beach, helping out at my uncle's farm, camping with the Scouts? Cuba was a great place to spend your childhood.

Today I have a memento from those early years, my Boy Scout uniform shirt. My Aunt Elvira brought it to me when she visited the United States many years later. The shirt shows that I had worked my way up to the rank of a First Class Boy Scout. I would have advanced further, but I never got the chance. Like so much else about my happy and comfortable life, the Scouts were suddenly and unexpectedly taken away from me.

The sheltered life I was living was about to change. *Everything* would soon change in Cuba.

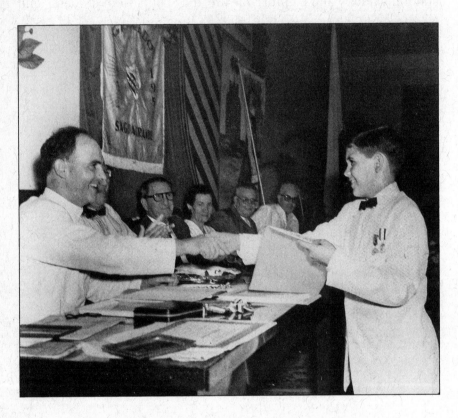

A REAL EDUCATION: Father Gayá, principal of my
Catholic school, one of my most important
mentors and the first to educate me in the
repressive ways of Communism.

Chapter 2

REVOLUTION

A T THE SOUND of machine-gun fire, Ralph and I dove to the ground.

Shots continued to ring out in the streets as my brother and I huddled together on the floor of our bedroom, seeking cover in the space between our two beds. Ralph, who was only seven years old, became so scared that his jaw shook uncontrollably. I knew I needed to comfort him, but truth be told, I was just as frightened.

It was April 1958, and a revolt was taking place in Cuba. Our house—and this bedroom in particular, since it was located in the center of the house—had for more than a day served as a bunker for our family. It wasn't just my brother and me taking refuge in the room; our parents were there as well, as were my grandmother Graciela and my aunt Graciela, my father's oldest sister, who had rushed out to our house on the outskirts of Sagua la Grande when revolutionaries took to the streets near their homes downtown. We were even providing a haven for one of the truck drivers from my family's soda company, who had showed up at our house earlier, desperate for shelter. He had had to abandon his truck when he came across fighting in the streets near our home. All of us stayed on the floor of the bedroom as the violence raged on outside.

The revolt was part of a revolutionary movement against Cuba's leader, General Fulgencio Batista, who had seized power in a coup in 1952. Cuba had never known long periods of stable democratic government. The closest thing to it was the period after the adoption of the 1940 Constitution, and Batista's coup ended this golden era abruptly. The gunshots we heard in Sagua were just the latest—and to us, the scariest—manifestation of the ever-growing opposition movement.

Many segments of the Cuban population were calling for democratic change. In recent months I had watched student and labor groups demonstrating and marching with banners past the windows of my grade school. I always found the unrest disturbing but I didn't realize how deep my fear could run until this armed revolt came so close to our home.

I had first known something more serious was going on earlier in the week when my parents decided to keep Ralph and me out of school. They had gotten word that anti-Batista forces, mostly young people, were organizing a general strike throughout Cuba to bring the country to a crippling halt. With the Batista forces fighting to hold on to power, my mom and dad knew the situation could get violent. So Ralph and I stayed home.

I didn't fully understand the gravity of the situation. I was only eleven years old, and I was more than happy to play outside with Ralph on this unplanned day off from school. But then, at around eleven o'clock on that first morning home, my mother came rushing out and hurried us back into the house, telling us we weren't to go outside again. Not long thereafter my grandmother and aunt showed up, hoping our house would be safer than their downtown location had been.

Moments later, my dad's car roared into the driveway. He dashed into the house out of breath. He seemed harried, even frantic.

That's when my parents decided to make Ralph's and my bedroom the family's safe zone, which only increased my nervousness. But I didn't realize how scared I really was until that afternoon, when we unexpectedly heard a knock on the door. Startled and scared, we watched my father go to answer it. It was not at all common to see my dad frightened, but he was clearly shaken as he answered the door.

It was the rebels. Except this group of young men—white, middle-class, typical anti-Batista youths—looked almost as afraid as we were. They were there to ask for my father's hunting shotgun. Apologetically, they tried to explain who they were and why they had to take his gun. My dad immediately said, "I don't want to know—just go!" He loved that 16-caliber pump action, and now it was a revolutionary arm.

It was on the second day that the violence escalated dramatically. Reinforcements for Batista's forces stormed into Sagua, and the sounds of gunfire grew louder and louder as they got closer to our home. Then, suddenly, the clatter of machine-gun fire exploded in our ears. This time we knew the fighting had come within just a few blocks of our formerly peaceful home. That is when Ralph and I jumped to the floor, petrified. For all we knew the gunfight would soon surround us.

Only later did we learn exactly what that eruption of gunfire was. Batista's soldiers had turned their overwhelming firepower on a house only a few blocks away from ours. Apparently they thought that someone had fired on them from inside the building. After the fighting ended, I looked at that house and could see that it had been pockmarked by bullets.

The Batista counteroffensive only intensified. From our front porch window we watched the Cuban Air Force B-27s strafing the rebels in the woods off in the distance. Days later, on one of my afternoon outings with Uncle Rinaldo at his farm, I stood in the craters made by the bombs and picked up .50-caliber shell casings from the standoff between the rebels and the government troops.

The anti-Batista forces' planned strike ultimately failed, and the government put down the revolt that had come so near to our house. But the fighting did not end there. Months later, while I was camping with my Boy Scout troop out in the woods, I heard more gunshots. The government troops and the rebels were at it again. As I listened to shots ringing out in the distance, I knew that I didn't even have the shelter of our house this time. We were out in the open. We felt helpless, and were kept awake through much of the night. Luckily the fighting did not approach us this time.

Life was changing. Bad things were happening on a more frequent basis. Just a kid, I had never imagined that such turmoil could rock our lives.

The revolution was under way, and gaining ground. It enjoyed great popular support, with the promise of free elections and an end to corruption. It was clear that the opposition had the Batista government on the run. When the United States government withdrew support for Batista, the end was inevitable.

It came on New Year's Eve in 1958. That night, Ralph and I were staying with my grandmother Graciela while our parents went to a New Year's Eve party. At the stroke of midnight we ate the traditional twelve grapes; this is an old and honored Cuban custom, with each grape symbolizing one of the twelve months of the coming year. Eating all twelve grapes is believed to bring to the household good luck and many blessings.

In this case, it wasn't to be.

We didn't realize it at the time, but just as we were getting into bed in those first hours of 1959, Batista and his entourage were boarding an airplane in Havana and flying into exile. The new year was not the only change we would face when we awakened in the morning. Our lives would never be the same again. We were starting the uncharted course of the revolution under Fidel Castro.

❖ ❖ ❖

ALTHOUGH THE PRECEDING years in Cuba had been turbulent, even violent, I had no inkling of what lay ahead for our country after Castro seized power. I was only twelve years old, a happy kid, and never really thought much about the future. The truth is, though, most people failed to anticipate the catastrophe that Castro would bring. Nobody could quite see how dramatically life would change.

Strange as it may sound now, to some people Castro seemed like a savior at the time. The new leader played to the Cuban people's hopes for the future—at first, anyway. The young, charismatic former lawyer put on a pretty good act as the romantic liberator, the enlightened leader. He vowed that he did not want power for himself. He proclaimed that he was not a Communist but a humanist. He promised open government and free elections within eighteen months.

That façade soon began to crack.

Although Castro spoke of noble intentions, in retrospect it is obvious that he was a tyrant from the start. He promptly put his brother, Raúl, in charge of the armed forces to make sure he stayed in power. And he immediately gave non-Cuban Che Guevara—an avowed Communist—a large role in the new government, the economy, and the treasury. These two power moves were clear markers of the true nature of his regime.

Castro was not an ordinary dictator; he was a Communist, an

ideology-driven dictator. There is a difference. Garden-variety dictators, dangerous as they are, are interested in graft, corruption, and
power, and little more. Under such a dictator, the people need to
keep their mouths shut and mind their own business, but if they do
so they are typically not bothered. Under a Communist dictator like
Castro the regime demands total compliance. Dissent can't be toler-
ated. Everyone has to conform or suffer the consequences.

This was the sort of suffocating control that Castro's Communist
regime was starting to impose in Cuba, affecting political power,
social conditions, economic systems.

Within a year of Castro's seizing power, reality had begun to set
in among the Cuban people. All around us we recognized ominous
signs that Castro was not simply a charismatic albeit radical leader.
He was consolidating his power as any dictator would. His promises
of democratic government and open elections were not materializ-
ing. He was cozying up to Soviet Russia, even as he denied being a
Communist.

For me, one of the earliest signs came when my dad arrived
home from work one day complaining that Castro's government
was taking people's land and farms without compensation. The Castro regime called this policy *intervención*. Making matters worse, the
agricultural authorities had begun slaughtering cattle—including
prize seed bulls worth a fortune in breeding potential. Castro's government, in other words, was forfeiting the future for a quick fix.

Cuba at the time had a pretty sophisticated cattle industry for a
country its size; as a matter of fact, Cuba was then one of the leading economies in Latin America. It exported cattle to Venezuela, and
as the veterinarian in Sagua my dad certified that the cattle were
healthy before they were exported. So he understood the cattle
industry and its importance to the Cuban people. And he was very

worried that the government's slaughtering would cause meat short-ages in our country.

Sure enough, the shortages appeared. The government eliminated the private sector and soon began to ration all food. It was gross mismanagement.

This was the agrarian revolution.

The problems have plagued Cuba ever since.

❖   ❖   ❖

MY EDUCATION AT Sagrado Corazón de Jesús, my Catholic ele-mentary school, exposed me to the dark realities of Communism. Many of the school's faculty members had come from Spain and were survivors of the Spanish Civil War. They knew the ways of a repressive system when it was trying to establish firm control over everything and everyone. And they did not hesitate to warn us about what was happening to Cuba. Even at a time when Fidel Cas-tro was denying that he was a Communist, the priests forthrightly— and correctly—explained that Communism had come to our country.

In particular, it was my mentor, Father Gayá, who described what that meant, what a Communist system did, and the damage it could do to the people. He told us stories about the cruelty of the Spanish Civil War and how the Communists (as he referred to them—they are better known as the Republican forces) had been so remarkably hostile to religion that they had killed priests. He also remembered that Communists in the Spanish Civil War had sent children to Russia for indoctrination, and some of those chil-dren never made it back to Spain. Father Gayá and the other priests understood how the Communists worked and acted. And their stunning stories about their firsthand experiences with the horrors of Communism had a profound impact on me, especially when they warned us so frankly that Cuba was now plagued with the same system.

But for me, nothing did more to open my eyes to the true nature of Communism than Castro's closing of all private and religious schools and his expulsion of priests and nuns from the country. Sagrado Corazón de Jesús had become in many ways the center of my life; it was where I learned, where I practiced my faith, where I had my friends, where I played. Then, practically overnight, it was all shut down—the school, the chapel, everything. Without warning our mentors and educators were sent away, kicked out of the country entirely. We never even got to say good-bye. There was nothing we could do. We felt powerless.

It was clear why the Castro government was threatened by the Catholic Church: the church was firm in its anti-Communism and formed a cohesive opposition to the ever more repressive government. To firm up his power, Castro simply had to get rid of this problem.

This turn of events showed me, on a deeply personal level, that a totalitarian ruler could take away your personal liberties in an instant. My Catholic faith was central to my life, and suddenly Castro had dictated that we were not to worship. My school and my teachers had shaped my identity, and suddenly Castro had torn them away. He was dictating what we could and could not do with our lives. Under Castro, no independence was left to the individual.

Sagrado Corazón de Jesús remained shuttered for the rest of my days in Cuba. Today this school is at the top of the list of things I long to see again. Nothing could have impressed this longing on me more clearly than a trip to Russia I made a few years ago while I was serving as secretary of Housing and Urban Development (HUD). In Saint Petersburg we visited the office from which Lenin had led the Revolution in 1917. The office was in a building that used to be a girls' school operated by nuns, and it immediately reminded me of my own school in Sagua la Grande. My hosts found it odd that my questions focused not on Lenin but on the dispossessed schoolgirls and nuns. I wondered how many of them got out safely.

❖   ❖   ❖

THE CLOSING OF my school and the expulsion of the priests turned me once and for all against the Communist regime. With Sagrado Corazón de Jesús closed, I had to attend the public high school in Sagua. In my time there I saw that the Communist regime was clearly shifting Cuba's schools away from the normal education mission—teaching reading and writing and math skills—to indoctrination. Our books were filled with Communist propaganda, with hostility to the Catholic Church, the United States, and the rich or the perceived rich.

It all became too much for me, even though I was just in my early teens. I became involved in clandestine protests against the Castro government. I was no underground hero, by any means; in these small protests I was joining many of my classmates at school. Typically this work amounted to passing along mimeographed sheets that contained information unflattering to Castro's regime, such as discussions of anti-Castro uprisings that were occurring in the mountains. Sheets would be placed at a particular page inside a dictionary in the school library, and I would go locate the book and pass along the mimeographed sheets to other kids in school. Or sometimes I'd be the one who put the sheets in the dictionary for someone else to retrieve.

This stealth work was driven by my strong sense of the damage Castro's government was doing to our country, but ultimately it was pretty insubstantial. My parents didn't think so, though. One day they found a mimeographed communiqué behind our large console radio in the living room. This discovery unhinged them. My parents realized that I had a certain unwillingness to bend to the system, and they worried that this would put me in danger in Cuba's new climate.

Their fears were well founded. A few months earlier, in April 1961, a group of Cuban exiles sponsored by the CIA had attempted— and failed—to overthrow Castro. This was the fiasco known as the Bay of Pigs invasion. The Communist government clamped down even more after the Bay of Pigs. Boys only slightly older than I was had gotten on the wrong side of the dictator and landed in prison. In one particularly nasty incident, Castro's soldiers seized a sixteen-year-old boy in Sagua named Mirabales and killed him by firing squad. The boy's sin? He had been caught transporting a rifle for the counterrevolutionary forces. The regime showed him no mercy, even though he was just a teenager who worked as a delivery boy for his family's floral business.

My parents feared I had the same hard core of rebelliousness in me and would meet the same fate.

❖　　❖　　❖

ONLY TWO YEARS after Fidel Castro rose to power, the changes that had come to Cuba were staggering. Far from being a savior, Castro had done extraordinary damage—he had collectivized farming, expropriated many industries and businesses both foreign and domestic, denied people the ability to worship or speak freely, closed schools and churches, expelled priests and nuns. In December 1961, he would make it official and declare himself to be a Marxist-Leninist.

In a flash, life had changed. People had to react quickly and radically. Desperation overwhelmed many families, including my own.

One evening in the spring of 1961, my parents called me into their bedroom. When they closed the door behind me, I knew that this would be a serious conversation. We had a maid at the house, and they didn't want her to hear. I sat down on the corner of their bed and my mom sat down next to me. My dad was standing off to the side.

They spoke softly but carefully. They said the time had come for me to leave Cuba.

This jolted me. It's not that leaving was completely unheard of. Some of my friends had told me they were considering it, and a few others had actually departed already. But for me it had never been more than idle curiosity. Suddenly my parents were making this all very real.

They said they would not force me to leave, but they thought it was the wise thing to do, even though it meant going by myself. They feared too much for my safety, especially because I was reaching the age when kids got into political trouble in Cuba. My younger brother, Ralph, would stay with them, as would my sister, Margarita, who had been born only a year earlier. But I needed to seize an opportunity to escape that they had heard about from a friend: a program run by the Catholic Church that was taking children out of Cuba to the United States. The program was very much an underground movement, they said, but it was my only chance at getting out.

I was just fourteen, and had never been apart from my family for anything longer than Boy Scout camping trips. Now they were urging me to go out on my own and leave the only country I had ever known.

I looked at my mother. She appeared saddened but determined. She wanted me safe in a better place, even though it would be a painful loss for her.

This was not the first I had heard of my parents' fears. The underground communiqué they found in our living room had obviously alarmed them. But I did not know what had convinced them that I absolutely had to leave.

They explained that the final straw had come as they watched one of my recent basketball games. I had played while wearing a scapular, which is a religious article made of cloth and worn around the neck like a medal. Displaying such tangible evidence of my faith was, I knew, controversial in Castro's Cuba, where the regime was cracking down on religious liberties. Wearing it was an act of defiance, an assertion of self, of choice, of freedom in the face of Communist indoctrination and persecution. But I did not realize how much it had riled a group of militiamen who were at the game. The very fact that there were militiamen at a high school basketball game is an indication of just how militarized Cuban society became under Castro.

The militiamen, my parents told me, had become obsessed with my scapular and had taunted me relentlessly. This was not mere heckling; it was vicious. "Kill him! Kill him!" the militiamen shouted. As an athlete, I had learned to tune out catcalls from the crowd, but my mom and dad heard every word. My parents now revealed that they had been terrified: "These people had guns," they told me. "They were yelling at you, saying, 'Get him! Get the Catholic!'" To my mom and dad, this was the crucial moment, when men with guns were shouting "Kill him!" about their teenage son. Given everything that Castro's regime had already done, these threats sounded all too real.

My parents said, "We feel the walls are closing in. This world is getting smaller; they are not tolerant of people like you. You will be in danger, and you are probably not going to conform to this system. You're not going to be happy living in it. You won't knuckle under to it, so you're going to be at risk."

I understood that my mother and father were not making a rash decision. Our behind-closed-doors meeting was, I realized, the culmination of a lengthy thought process. Ultimately they had concluded that leaving was the only smart and safe thing for me to do. They were committed to fighting through whatever red tape they had to in order to try to get me out.

What would happen to my parents and my siblings? Although they could not leave with me now, my parents told me that they might follow. But it was more likely, they said, that I would return after Castro was ousted by the United States. At that point my dad felt sure that things would change for the better, that Castro would not last. Even after the Bay of Pigs failure, my dad's rallying cry was that the United States would not permit a Communist government ninety miles from its shore. My exile, we all hoped, would be temporary. But in the meantime there would be upheaval, and my parents wanted to ensure that I was protected from it.

I understood the magnitude of what they were saying. I understood that this plan would mean being separated from my family, my friends, and my homeland. But I also understood that it was the only option. I told my parents I was very willing to go.

Now it became a kind of clandestine operation. My parents told me it had to be carried out in total secrecy. I must not tell anyone about it, or else the opportunity could be lost forever.

The escape plan was in motion.

A FINAL CELEBRATION: Exactly two months
before I fled Cuba, our family celebrated
Margarita's first birthday.

Chapter 3

EXIT STRATEGY

W ITHIN A FEW days of the hushed discussion in my parents' bedroom, I had to travel to Havana for an important meeting. I needed to speak with the people who
could arrange my exit to the United States.

This program, which the Catholic Church and the U.S. State
Department had created in 1960 to allow Cuban children to escape
to freedom, was later known as Operation Peter Pan—or Pedro Pan,
in Spanish. With the help of my father's sister Luisa, my family had
had some long-distance contact with the program's coordinators in
Havana. Now it was necessary to meet with them face-to-face. So as
not to arouse any suspicion, my parents did not go with me. They
put me on a train from Sagua la Grande to the Cuban capital, more
than two hundred miles away. It was the first time in my life I traveled alone.

Aunt Luisa picked me up when I got to the Havana train station.
Our family had taken yearly trips to Havana, but they were nothing
like this. As soon as I met Luisa, she took me to an extremely beautiful home in the heart of Havana. Looking back now, I realize it was

one of the classic old Havana homes, probably on Quinta Avenida, in the city's glamorous section.

Aunt Luisa brought me inside, into a big front room. There I was introduced to several women and one man. These were the people I had come to meet. They asked me a number of questions. It was a friendly exchange, though I can't recall specifics of what they asked or how I answered. They did, however, strike me as incredibly nice and helpful people. And one thing above all else I can recall vividly: as I walked out of that beautiful Havana house at the end of the meeting, I knew that these people were going to help get me out of Cuba.

❖   ❖   ❖

THAT INTERVIEW SET the wheels in motion, but getting out of the country would not happen quickly. There was too much red tape, too much paperwork. For starters, I needed to get a passport. On the surface that process was routine, since Cubans at the time could apply to the government to leave the country for up to thirty days. But I knew that with the Peter Pan program, this was anything but routine. We had to keep my real reason for leaving a complete secret; I couldn't discuss it with anyone. My parents and I had to take care of many other details as well. There was, for example, the matter of getting my visa to enter the United States, which the Catholic Church in Miami was providing.

My parents wanted me to be as prepared as possible to live on my own. So they took me shopping. My mother bought me a small leather pouch for all the documents I would need for traveling. My parents also took me to J. Vallé, a fine men's store in Havana, to buy two wool suits, one blue, one brown. They felt I needed to be well outfitted in clothes. What we didn't realize was that the suits would be unnecessary in the places I would be going in America. My mom and dad even thought they were helping me prepare by signing me up for English lessons. The tutor was a wonderful gentleman we called Mr. George. The trouble was that as a Jamaican immigrant, he had an accent that was definitely not American. What I picked up in the few short months I worked with Mr. George would prove to be worthless when I got to America.

More than anything else, it became a waiting game. Even after we knew that I had been approved for the Peter Pan program, we had no idea *when* I would be leaving. We were told that I would receive a telegram when a flight opened up, but we'd receive only about two days' warning and would then have to rush to Havana to catch the plane. This was an anxious time, and must have been agonizing for my parents.

By this point I was no longer in school. Castro had shut down my Catholic school, of course, but I wasn't even attending the public high school in Sagua that I had gone to for a while. My parents had decided to hold me out to spare me from Communist indoctrination. I was idle, just hanging around waiting for that precious telegram to show up.

That's when I made the foolish decision that nearly cost me my ticket out of Castro's Cuba.

In January 1962, a bunch of my friends decided to attend a tryout for the Cuban swimming team that would compete in the Pan American Games. Unbeknownst to my parents, I tagged along. I was not a great swimmer by competitive standards, but I had spent a lot of time in the water at Playa Uvero every summer. So at the tryout I just jumped into the water and swam. I didn't think much of it at the time.

A few weeks later I received a telegram. My parents and I at first thought it was the message we had been desperately waiting for, the one telling me that I could finally leave the country. Instead it was a telegram summoning me to report to the Sports Palace in Havana to try out for the national swimming team. Though I was an untrained swimmer, I guess they liked my size. I was tall and lanky.

This telegram scared my parents to death. They knew that the Castro government emphasized sports heavily and restricted the athletes it recruited, watching them constantly.

"What did you do?" my parents said. "Now they're looking for you. They won't let you leave now, because they want you for the Pan American Games in Panama."

Me, I thought it would be great to go to Panama. I was thinking like the kid I was, eager to compete in athletics and ready to see another part of the world. But my parents reminded me of the danger I had created with my carelessness.

We took a chance and I didn't report for the swimming tryout on the assigned date. And I got incredibly lucky: right about the time of the tryout, the long-awaited telegram arrived telling me that my flight would be leaving from Havana for Miami.

It was a close call. Too close, for my parents.

❖   ❖   ❖

When the day came to leave Sagua la Grande, my dad couldn't bear to see me off at the airport. I said good-bye to him outside my grandmother Graciela's house in the center of Sagua. When we walked outside, we stood on the sidewalk under the apartment's balcony. It was nearly the same spot where he had put me on the bus for my first day of school many years before. Back then my father had made sure to instruct me to say good morning to the bus driver. Now words were harder to come by. He simply squeezed my arm, not letting go. Finally, after a long silence, he said softly, "I'll see you in three months."

That was all he could manage to get out of his mouth. Saying good-bye to him wasn't any easier for me. The moment was charged for both of us. For months he had talked to me, counseled me, schooled me in what to expect, not just when I arrived in America, but in life in general. During the time that the plans took shape for me to leave, my dad and I fell into a natural ritual. It was totally spontaneous. At bedtime, he would go into his room and stretch out on the bed. I would walk in and lie down beside him. For twenty minutes, maybe half an hour each night, we just talked, the two of us stretched out on the bed, staring at the ceiling, imagining the future, him talking, me listening. I wish I could recount everything he said, but I can't. I was too young and unaware of its great significance to memorize it. Still, I absorbed it subconsciously. It became part of me. It was intelligent, instructive, full of insight and wisdom. It went into my heart, my soul, my blood. It wasn't just for the head. It was spiritual too, a whole philosophy of how to handle whatever life threw at you. He talked about values to live by—honesty, doing your best, friendship, loyalty.

Now, standing under my grandmother's balcony, we were parting ways. Unable to find a satisfactory way to say good-bye to the man who meant so much to me, I simply turned away, got into the car with my mother, brother, and uncle Eduardo, and left for Havana.

❖   ❖   ❖

WHEN WE ARRIVED in Havana we stayed at Aunt Luisa's house for two days, doing last-minute paperwork and ensuring that everything was in order. We left my aunt's house early on the morning of February 6, 1962, and headed toward José Martí Airport, in Rancho Boyeros, just outside Havana. Until then the airport had been just a name in the news to me—I had never flown before and had no idea what to expect. I was to leave on the afternoon flight, one of two Pan American flights daily between Miami and Havana. Flight 442, I believe it was.

Since there was a sixty-pound weight limit on luggage, we had crammed my clothes into a big, lightweight duffel bag rather than the heavy Samsonite suitcases that were the alternative in those days. Everybody used these duffel bags, called *gusanos,* meaning "worms." In fact, so many Cubans fled the country with these big bags that looked like gigantic worms that Castro began to use the term *gusanos* as a pejorative for counterrevolutionaries and exiles.

Soon after checking my bag with the airline, I found myself in the *pecera,* the glass room that held all passengers before departure. Like all other passengers, I would be forced to wait several hours in this "fishbowl" before I could leave. Most of that time was spent simply waiting. I knew I would be summoned into another room to be interrogated by authorities of the Castro government. These officials, in their olive uniforms, called passengers in one by one, checking and rechecking all documents. During this inspection process they strip-searched some passengers, including even children much younger than I.

I was fortunate to escape this demeaning treatment. In fact, the only problem I encountered related to my family's telephone bill. Even though my parents were not leaving Cuba, the authorities wanted the bill paid up. I was allowed to get cash from my family on the other side of the glass. The bill was something like twenty-seven pesos—not a lot of money even then—but my uncle Eduardo gave me a lot more as a way of "smoothing" the issue.

Other than that contact with Uncle Eduardo, I was separated from my family the entire time I was sequestered in the *pecera.* The time spent there was excruciatingly difficult. I could see my family through the glass divide, but I couldn't hear anything they said or reach out to them for a comforting hug or pat on the arm. It was as if this was a precursor to the agonizing years of separation to come.

Finally the time came to board the Pan Am DC-6 that would take me away from Cuba and to the United States. I had no idea what lay ahead of me, but I could look back to the glass wall of the *pecera* to see what I was leaving behind.

As I climbed the stairs into that airplane in Havana, I gave a final glance back at my family members, who remained on the other side of the glass. That's when I made eye contact with my mother one last time. I could see the pain written on her face. It was an acute reminder of the dramatic and frightening transition I was about to make. To this day, that desperate look on my mother's face is emblazoned in my memory; I will carry it with me to the grave.

That was the last time I ever set foot in Cuba.

REFUGEE: When I arrived in America I lived in
two different camps for Cuban refugee boys.
Here I am at Camp St. John in Jacksonville
(I am lying in the top bunk).

Chapter 4

EXILE

IMMIGRANT, REFUGEE, EXILE.

This is what I became when our DC-6 took off from Havana en route to Miami. I was fifteen years old, and my entire world, the normal and the familiar, was gone.

I was not the only child from Operation Peter Pan embarking on a new life. There were eleven of us on that plane, I believe. Many of the children were younger than me; some were as young as nine or ten years old.

That flight, as you might imagine, was filled with anxiety. Seated next to me was a girl, about eleven years old, who was extremely anxious. I was scared and nervous as well, but I did my best to console her. I was older, so it seemed that it was my responsibility to help her. It also just felt natural at the time. We had been thrown into this bewildering experience together; we should get through it together. I spoke to her through the entire flight, trying to soothe her.

I remember my interactions with that girl vividly, but years later I learned that apparently I consoled other kids as well. One came up to me and thanked me formally. Another person wrote and informed

me, "I was on the flight with you and you're the guy who helped me."
A third individual told me that I had been kind to a good friend of
his who was on my flight. This ongoing interaction among children
of the Peter Pan program is not unusual; a bond was being formed
by our experiences as exiles in America.

As nervous as we all were, we had an opportunity to release some
of our tension when the pilot announced that we had left Cuban air-
space. The plane erupted in a loud cheer. All of us were leaving our
home and looking for the safety and security of the United States.

We landed in Miami as the sun was setting. I was only ninety
miles from Cuba, but the life I was about to begin was a world away
from the one I had known in Sagua la Grande.

As I walked off the plane and onto the tarmac, surrounded by
kids fighting panic, I felt waves of anxiety myself. My father had
prepared me for my new fears. Whenever you make a bold move in
life, doubts assail you, he told me. But as much as I knew that coming to America was the right move, I was now overwhelmed by second thoughts about the decision to leave Cuba.

There I was, fifteen years old, standing in the Miami airport,
clutching my *gusano,* and it hit me: I was alone.

The U.S. Immigration officer quickly asked for children traveling by themselves. Those of us from the Peter Pan program were set
aside. It only reinforced the feeling that we kids were all alone in
America. The friends, the grandparents, the aunts, uncles, brothers,
sisters, and parents who had meant everything to us—all gone.

In fact, the only person I knew in the United States was a second
cousin, Manuel Mesa, who had already fled Cuba and was now living with an aunt in Miami. Manolito, as we knew him, had spent a
couple of summers at the beach with us, and he and I were close in
age. There at the airport was Manolito—dressed in his white shirt,
black pants, and bow tie from Winn-Dixie, where he was a bag

boy—welcoming me to America. He had to go back to work right away, but I was touched when he told me that he had simply wanted to make sure he saw me come in. Feeling adrift, I saw any connection to home as a lifeline.

❖   ❖   ❖

A GROUP OF volunteer workers for the Peter Pan program came to the airport to greet me and the other children who had arrived from Cuba. These volunteers, all Cubans, were wonderfully helpful, but I could not forget that they were strangers, every last one of them.

We were divided up by age, and four or five of us who were over the age of fourteen were shepherded into a van. I sat up front, next to the driver and watched through the big windshield as we drove out of the airport complex and sped onto the freeway. We were heading toward what would be our temporary quarters, an intake processing camp south of Miami. The driver was a nice man, but I remained silent as we drove along, engaging in no conversation. I was tired and needed to think, and I simply stared into the night, into the glare of white headlights and red taillights stretched out in front of us on the freeway. As the van's headlights illuminated the freeway's overhead signs, I read over and over this one recurring word: "Ahead." I did not know what it meant, which in retrospect seems entirely appropriate: I had no idea what lay ahead, what my future would hold.

When we reached the camp, known as Camp Matecumbe, we were led into a small cabin at what I would discover was the front of the property. There the director of the camp, Father Palá, put us through an intake interview. He made a three-by-five index card for each of us. It listed our name, our address in Cuba, our parents' names, our date of birth, and various other essential facts.

I fell asleep waiting for my turn to give the information to

Father Palá. I was not the only one. Nervous and disoriented though we were, we were exhausted. It was late, and it had been a long day. As soon as Father Palá finished with the last interview, we were gently shaken awake and loaded back into the van, which drove us deeper into the camp.

We were led into the dining hall—quietly, so as not to wake the other campers—and were each given a little carton of milk and an oatmeal raisin cookie. I had never eaten an oatmeal raisin cookie before but it's been my favorite ever since. I was ready for the milk, even though in Cuba we drank ours warm and with coffee. My great-uncle Mariano, who had lived in Key West, had told me that Americans drank cold milk. So for months prior to leaving Cuba I practiced being an American by drinking my milk cold. Some of the other kids at Matecumbe were thrown off by the carton of cold milk, but it was one of the few aspects of life I was prepared for in this new and strange world.

Matecumbe was meant to be a way station, and it was over-crowded. I later learned that more than four hundred kids were there when I arrived. That night they set us up on cots right there in the cafeteria. I was issued nothing but a rough and itchy Army sur-plus blanket—no pillows, no sheets. The February air in Miami seemed colder than anything I had ever experienced in Cuba, and I could not keep warm. I went to sleep wearing the same brand-new brown suit I had had on all day.

As I stretched out on that cot I thought, "Where am I?" and "What's going on?" A few minutes earlier, as we kids ate our cookie and sipped our milk, we had passed a few remarks among us in Spanish, but mostly we were quiet, no doubt the result of feeling so disoriented and so tired. Exhausted and scared, I fell back on what my mother had taught me: I said my bedtime prayers. I started to recite my three Hail Marys but I can't be sure I made it all the way through them. I only know that I fell asleep fast.

❖   ❖   ❖

EVERY DAY AT Matecumbe was a hard day. After our first night spent in the cafeteria, we were transferred to the largest of the camp's three cabins, which was for the new arrivals. Because of the increasing number of desperate families in the hell that Cuba had become, more and more children arrived in this cabin daily. The bunk beds were triple-tiered. The guy on the top had the vent from the heaters right on him, but the bottom got no heat at all. I was on the bottom. The bunks were so close together that if your neighbor coughed, you could feel it. In a camp surrounded by pine trees, we felt as though we were in the middle of nowhere.

But the physical conditions, though not luxurious by any means, were at least adequate. There were bigger problems, among them sheer boredom: we had nothing to do. We weren't going to school, since the plan was to move us out of the intake camp quickly. Sure, the camp administrators tried to find things we could do to pass the time. I found some distraction in the baseball games they arranged, which were played on a crude, rocky field. I also enjoyed the dances they coordinated with girls from nearby Camp Homestead, as they gave me a chance to catch up with some girls I had known back in Sagua. But overall our days were aimless; I felt adrift.

This feeling was intensified because the whole camp was transient. I was simply unable to settle in and be at ease, and I had none of the support network I was accustomed to. Even when political unrest came to Cuba and life became more dangerous and uncertain, my family was constantly there to lend support. But Matecumbe was a lonely place. With kids constantly moving in and out, I knew no one and had no connection to anything. I realized quickly that I was on my own. There was no parent to fall back on, no mother to comfort me. The psychological adjustment was taxing.

The sense of isolation was so powerful that I clung to any link to home I could find, no matter how tenuous. I discovered that a Cuban man working as a janitor at the camp had known my dad in Cuba. They had gone bird hunting together. I would talk to this man every chance I got. That was only occasionally, for just a few short minutes at a time. But this kind man provided me with a much-needed anchor.

An even more important lifeline was being able to speak to my parents on the telephone. On Saturdays we were taken by school bus to Bayfront Park (Parque de las Palomas to Cuban exiles) in downtown Miami. On the first Saturday, I called home from a pay phone in the lobby of Miami's Americano Hotel. What a thrill it was to talk to my father and mother, even for just the few minutes we could manage. The first thing they asked, naturally, was how I was doing, and despite my loneliness and unhappiness at the crowded camp, I stayed upbeat, since I didn't want to cause them any additional worry. That, as it turned out, would be the pattern I followed in virtually all my communications with my parents. In that initial phone call even the simplest reminder of home was a great salve for me; our conversation was all about my situation and how soon I might move out of Matecumbe. It was short and to the point. For days afterward I relived that brief conversation in my head as I coped with my homesickness. When I think back on that now, as a father, I can only imagine the pain my parents must have felt in such an uncertain circumstance.

To help push me through at Matecumbe, I held on to the last words my father had said to me when I left Sagua: "I'll see you in three months." He had told me that he thought our separation would last no more than ninety days, and had encouraged me to look at those three months as a chance to learn English. Papi's ninety-day estimate gave me hope. His other words of advice gave me strength; I thought back constantly to our daily talks in my final months in Cuba, the wisdom he had imparted to me as we lay together on his bed.

One factor above all others sustained me in these disorienting, dispiriting early days in America. In the many years since, I have been asked over and over, "How did you survive on your own as a fifteen-year-old exile in a foreign country whose language you didn't speak?" My answer is always the same: "My faith."

My family and my schooling in Cuba had instilled in me a deep belief and faith in God. I had learned the concept of Divine Providence and knew that God looked after those who kept their covenant with him and looked to him for guidance. My faith became a tremendous resource at a time when I felt helpless and lost. My religion came strongly to the fore. Every night I'd say those three bedtime Hail Marys. That was a constant in my life. I also attended mass daily at the camp. Every morning Father Palá, the camp director, would say mass in a little cabin that was a combination office and improvised chapel. These morning masses reminded me of the chapel back at school in Cuba, where we'd attend mass at the beginning of every school day.

At this juncture my faith was the only hope I had. It pulled me through. It was the sole antidote to the overwhelming feelings of homesickness, loneliness, and confusion. Those first few months in America were painful for me, and I could only imagine how rough they were for the younger kids. I know for certain that many a tear was shed in those cabins at night after lights-out. Many of the younger kids must have felt abandoned by their parents, too young to comprehend why their families had sent them to a different country.

I was lucky in that regard. At age fifteen, I was old enough to know for sure that my parents had their own agony to shoulder over this separation from me. There was no possibility that they had abandoned me. Their sacrifice was excruciating too. I had merely to remember my father's emotional farewell under my grandmother's balcony in Sagua or to conjure the image of my mother's distraught face at the airport in Havana to summon their pain. Even then, though, it took becoming a parent myself, many years later, to be able to realize fully the love and hope for me that had guided my parents' decision to send me out of an increasingly chaotic life in Cuba.

❖   ❖   ❖

FATHER BRYAN WALSH was the founder of the Peter Pan program. At this point I had never met or even seen this Catholic priest; he was just a larger-than-life figure whose name we heard mentioned all the time. He was not around Matecumbe much, for the simple reason that he was too busy administering what he had created. He was responsible for resettling fourteen thousand of us kids in roughly a year and a half. Father Walsh devoted his time to placing all these children in other camps, in orphanages, or in foster homes all over the country.

I knew I would be moved out of Camp Matecumbe, and from the beginning my great hope was that I would go to Camp St. John in Jacksonville, Florida. After several days at Matecumbe, my turn came to meet with a social worker, and I explained my desire to be transferred to Jacksonville. Some kids I knew from Cuba were already at Camp St. John, and a distant relative of my dad's, a wonderful lady named Araceli Lopez, nicknamed Cuquita, lived in Jacksonville and was a volunteer at the camp. Actually, I assumed that sending me to Camp St. John was a done deal, since Cuquita was doing all she could to make it happen, and several of the kids I knew at the camp were requesting that I be sent there as well.

When I met with the social worker, she said in a very flat and cold way, "You're not going to Camp St. John. We're not sending any more kids there. The place is full." She told me the likely placements for me would be in either Albuquerque, New Mexico, or a nice town in Nebraska.

Albuquerque? Nebraska? I couldn't even place them on a map, though I knew Albuquerque was out West somewhere, probably from some western I'd seen in the Teatro Encanto in Sagua. It didn't matter where these places were. I didn't want to go there. I wanted to go to Jacksonville and stay in Florida.

Everything came crashing down at this moment. I hit bottom. I was desperate. I felt very alone, and I kept wondering what the future held, what lay *"Ahead."*

Years later Father Walsh, by then Monsignor Walsh, gave me the file the Peter Pan program kept on me during my time under its care. There was a notation in the file from this social worker that I was despondent and very upset that I could not go to Jacksonville. That was probably putting it mildly. I have a feeling that looking across her desk, she could spot my despair instantly.

Cuquita ended up saving me. She knew the church hierarchy well and intervened on my behalf. Days later I was called back to the front office and learned that I would be going to Jacksonville after all. When I found out, I was overjoyed. The camp had a fun tradition in which those leaving would be thrown in the swimming pool, but I was so excited I got ahead of the tradition: when I got back from the office I jumped right in, fully clothed.

Finally, on March 16, after forty long days at Camp Matecumbe, I was sent off to Camp St. John, the next step in my journey to becoming an American.

❖   ❖   ❖

MY SPIRITS IMPROVED as soon as I got to Camp St. John, which was in a beautiful setting on the banks of the St. Johns River. One reason was that I was now with three boys I knew. Two boys, the Leorza brothers, were actually from Sagua la Grande, and thus formed an important link to home. The third, Cesar Calvet, a year my senior, had lived in Havana but had often visited his relatives in Sagua, where his parents had grown up. I had known him only slightly in Cuba, but we became much better acquainted in America. In fact, Cesar and I would become lifelong friends.

Another reason I was happy to be assigned to Camp St. John was that it was more settled, and less crowded. Instead of more than four hundred boys, there were only seventy of us. Whereas Matecumbe was strictly in and out, with massive turnover, the camp in Jacksonville was less transient. There was a sense of community, because the kids there had been living together for quite some time. At Camp St. John life was more social, less disorienting, and far more fulfilling, and friendships were formed in that camp that have lasted to this day, like mine with Cesar. The first night in Jacksonville I was able to get Cesar to place a call to my parents from a pay phone by the dining hall; I couldn't do it myself because I didn't know English well enough to speak to the operator. All I could do was let my parents know that I was out of Matecumbe and at Camp St. John. Other than that kind of sporadic communication by proxy, I was completely out of touch with my family. Only later would I start receiving letters, and they would typically take more than a month to arrive.

As had been the case at Matecumbe, not a word of English was spoken at Camp St. John. Nor would I be forced to learn the language right away, since I had arrived in Jacksonville too late in the school year to be enrolled in Bishop Kenny, the local Catholic high school that other boys from the camp attended. To give the fifteen or sixteen of us who had just arrived something to do, Camp St. John enrolled us in the adult education school in downtown Jacksonville. We would attend the English classes there and then roam the city park nearby. Eventually we would find our way to a bench, sit down and eat our bag lunch, then wait for the bus to take us back to camp. I began to learn some English, but it was minimal.

One night at Camp St. John I was awakened from a deep sleep by laughter and whispering. My top bunk was by the door. A group of girls from Bishop Kenny had launched a night raid on the camp so they could see their boyfriends. Our counselors quickly ran them off, but it was a rare moment of lighthearted fun during this time of serious adjustment. It also marked my first encounter with English-speaking American girls. None of them had come to see me, but the incident was such good fun that I thought maybe I could get used to life in America after all.

For entertainment in Jacksonville we had pickup baseball and basketball games. As we all got to know one another, we relied on alliances formed in past games when choosing up sides. It made for nice rivalries. One of the really fun experiences at Camp St. John was going to the games of the Jacksonville Suns, a minor-league baseball team. The church got free tickets for us in the right-field bleachers, next to the Suns' bullpen. We used to chat with a young Cuban pitcher who later became much better known as he made it in the majors. It was none other than Luis Tiant, a future All-Star.

We also had a television set in the dining room. It was the first television set I had seen that "spoke English." On Saturday afternoons I would often watch baseball games with a handful of other boys. But I would only watch, because I didn't yet understand enough English to follow the commentary from the two announcers, Hall of Famers Pee Wee Reese and Dizzy Dean. A year or so later, when my English had improved, I was able to enjoy their colorful byplay.

❖   ❖   ❖

WHEN I LOOK back I am so grateful that I was able to go to Camp St. John. Years later I read the award-winning memoir *Waiting for Snow in Havana,* written by fellow Peter Pan alumnus Carlos Eire, now a professor of religion and history at Yale. He was sent from the transient camp at Matecumbe to live with a foster family in Chicago, and I know from his account of living there that the adjustment was quite a bit more difficult for him, especially with the long and brutal winters and the scarcity of fellow Cuban exiles. I, on the other hand, lucked out and spent about three months at the camp in Jacksonville and formed fast friends there. We were not isolated and alienated as we had been at Camp Matecumbe. We were no longer just being processed. We were like a brotherhood. We banded together.

So when word leaked out late in May that the camp would be closing in a couple of weeks and we would be placed with foster families, we were angry. For me this would mean my third new home in four months. It was the same for many of the other boys at the camp. We said, "What are you doing to us? What are you thinking? We're fine here. We're okay, we're happy. Leave us alone. Don't move us, whatever you do!"

Our cries fell on deaf ears. We had to leave that camp. We had to make a really scary move, into the American mainstream. We would be living with strangers, all of them Americans, all of them speaking only one language, English. We would become part of a truly foreign and scary unknown—an American family.

Our Catholic Charities social worker at the camp was Tom Aglio, a young man who, because of his Boston accent, I was convinced was speaking something other than English. For weeks before Mr. Aglio announced to us that Camp St. John would be closing, he had been painstakingly working to find and screen the foster homes to which we would be sent. A plea was made at Sunday masses throughout the Diocese of St. Augustine, which in those days covered all of Florida except the southeast. As an adult, I have marveled at the generosity of spirit of the families who volunteered. They were agreeing to take into their homes teenaged boys from a country they did not know, about whom they knew nothing, and who in many cases (including mine) did not speak their language. And they were agreeing to do so for an undetermined period of time. That is truly faith in action.

When it became clear to Mr. Aglio that the camp would be shut down, he arranged for a group picture to be taken of all of us boys as a souvenir of our time there. This simple act of having a camp photo taken caused me a great deal of concern. I was terrified that the Cuban regime would discover that I was in the Peter Pan program and would threaten the safety of my family. So I purposely avoided showing my face in the photo. What now seems so silly on my part has been a lifelong reminder to me of what a repressive tyrant can do to people, especially to impressionable young people.

❖   ❖   ❖

MY FATHER HAD said we'd be reunited after three months, but those ninety days came and went. Now, as I was about to move to a

HIDING: The boys of Camp St. John. Only the top of my head is visible *(back row)* because I feared that Cuba's Communist regime would punish my family if it discovered I had escaped to America.

foster home, I had to face the fact that I no idea when I might see my parents again. I held out hope, however. My spirits were raised when I got a piece of great news: my brother Ralph, now twelve years old, had made it to America. He had arrived in Miami toward the end of my time at Camp St. John, along with Aunt Luisa; her husband, Mario; and their daughters, Luisita and Margarita. I was overjoyed to be in this country with my brother, even though we were still separated by more than two hundred miles. His presence in America gave me hope for the future.

My American family: At a lakeside party with
my foster families, the Youngs and the
Berkmeyers, the week I arrived in Orlando. *From
left to right:* Jim Berkmeyer's mother and father,
Jim Berkmeyer, Eileen Young (Tía), June
Berkmeyer, Cesar Calvet, me, and Jimmy Young
(sitting on the ground).

Chapter 5

HOMECOMING

CHANGE IS DIFFICULT. Some people can scarcely tolerate it. In Camp St. John we boys had formed a little community, a safe world. We shared a common heritage and we spoke a common language—the one we'd grown up speaking. The sound of it was comforting. As strangers in a strange land we had enough wrenching change to process without losing the close company of one another. Or so we thought. None of us wanted to lose the camaraderie we had. But we were wrong to resist assimilation and integration into the American way of life. The people in charge were right to decide we had to break up our old gang and insert ourselves into the lives of typical American families. Still, we didn't like it. We felt threatened by it.

I didn't speak English. The American family I was going to live with didn't speak Spanish. I'd never even known an American person to sit down and have a conversation with. As a boy I had listened to stories about America told by my great-uncle Mariano, whose time living in Key West had given him a facility in basic English, but that was it. I was going into an American family virtually inarticulate. Uncle Mariano had never had to live with an American family.

For me it was like going to Mars to live with Martians. It was an odd and intimidating prospect.

Easing my nerves slightly was the discovery that I was slated to move into the same foster home as my buddy Cesar Calvet. We would live together as de facto brothers. But at the last minute that arrangement unraveled when the foster parents, June and Jim Berkmeyer, realized that two teenage boys might be one too many. Only Cesar would live with them. I was back on my own.

I left Camp St. John on June 12, 1962. That day, twelve of us got onto a Greyhound bus headed to Orlando. We called ourselves the "Twelve Apostles." At the Orlando bus station our foster families were waiting to meet us. This led to the usual sort of confusion these convergences generate. Each kid had a piece of paper with the name of the family he was going to live with. The Peter Pan volunteers were directing traffic, saying, "You go over there." Or, "You belong with these nice people." Or, "Come over here. This is your new family." People moved in and out of my field of vision, until suddenly I saw before me my foster family, the Youngs. Standing there was a woman roughly the same age as my own mother, along with her two boys, who looked to be about my age.

I still felt more than a tinge of disappointment that I would not be with Cesar and the Berkmeyers, but the Youngs could not have been more open and welcoming. As soon as I met the mother, Eileen Young, I sensed that she was a take-charge person, yet also very gentle. Of French Canadian descent, Mrs. Young was not familiar with my name, Melquiades. She put her hand on my shoulder reassuringly and said, "Well, Melquiades is not going to do. Is it okay with you if we call you Mel?"

Although I didn't know English, I somehow understood what she meant. At home in Cuba they called me Melquiadito, "little Melquiades." But here in America I was going to be just plain Mel. I could handle that, I concluded on the spot. So I practically exhausted my knowledge of English and said, "Okay."

And with that, I got a new name, the name by which I would forever be known in America. But I always kept my name, Melquiades; I'm very proud of it.

Mrs. Young introduced me to her two sons. The older boy, Jimmy, was exactly my age. The younger one, Dennis, was a couple of years younger. We milled about at the bus station for only a short time more, saying good-bye to the other kids, and then we climbed into the family car and drove off. I immediately missed my friends from the camp, especially Cesar. Unable to speak English, I could not really talk with the Youngs, so I felt awkward and out of sorts.

The car pulled up to a small, plain house. Though it certainly was not fancy, I found it to be clean and comfortable. Mrs. Young, very solicitous of me, did her best to overcome the unavoidable awkwardness. So she brought out the natural thing, food. Without asking, she assumed the safest thing to give a fifteen-year-old boy was a peanut-butter-and-jelly sandwich. There was only one problem: I had never seen or heard of butter from peanuts. At first sight, peanut butter just didn't look like something you ate. Well, I did eat it, and after a short adjustment period, it would become my favorite sandwich.

By then my new foster father, Walter Young, had come home from work. He worked as a parts buyer for Martin Marietta, the big defense contractor. He was a quiet man but had a ready smile, and he put me at ease as well. Having settled the question of what I would be called, we needed to figure out how I would address these two new people who were acting in loco parentis. I had been brought up with good manners in Cuba—hence my father's instructing me on my first day of school to greet the bus driver and other adults with a hearty *"Buenos días."* I knew to address the adult volunteers in the Peter Pan program as "Mr." or "Mrs." or as "Sir" or "Madam." But what was I going to do with Mr. and Mrs. Young? It didn't feel right to call them Eileen and Walter. It was too familiar and smacked a bit of disrespect.

Mrs. Young asked me what I thought. I said, "Mom and Dad?"

"No," she said gently, "your mom and dad are in Cuba."

She resolved the matter with an aplomb that I soon learned was characteristic. She asked me how you said "aunt" and "uncle" in Spanish. I told her *"tía"* and *"tío."* She smiled and said, "That settles it then, Mel. You call us Tía and Tío."

This touched me. In fact, I started to cry—as did Mrs. Young. I knew I was lucky to be with this caring and sensitive family. I had my real mother and father trapped at home in Cuba, and I would have found calling others "Mom" and "Dad" a constant and painful reminder of their absence. Also, I remained hopeful that I would be reunited with my parents very soon. I did not want to slight them. So Mr. and Mrs. Young became Tío and Tía.

Decades later, in the last years of her life, Mrs. Young recalled this incident during one of our many chats. She said that she had known it would have pained me to call someone other than my parents "Mom" and "Dad," but that she had been impressed that I would have done so to make the situation work. She told me, "You were strong enough to do what you had to do, but relieved when you didn't have to."

❖   ❖   ❖

THE YOUNGS' HOUSEHOLD was crowded. Amazingly, Jimmy, the older son, gave me his bedroom and started sleeping on the couch in the family room. I have never forgotten his selfless act. The Youngs were spectacular in a thousand little ways like that. The adjective "generous" doesn't begin to do the family justice. They made me feel comfortable in their home, which is no small feat. Mrs. Young was incredibly supportive and nurturing, while Mr. Young was always kind. He was not gregarious and talkative the way my own father was, but he treated me very well and entertained all of us with his guitar and harmonica playing.

The two boys were great to me. During that first summer they took me around and showed me the neighborhood. Jimmy and I, being the same age, went to events and activities together, and many of his friends became my friends.

The Young boys and I had a terrific relationship, though we never became bosom buddies. That was probably better. They didn't have to feel obligated to take me with them everywhere and see that I was okay. It also forced me to forge my own identity and friendships. Making friends has never been hard for me, because I like people a lot. I got a chance to make new friends when school started at the end of the summer. I went to Bishop Moore, the Catholic school, while Jimmy and Dennis attended Evans High School, the public school. Part of the pledge to our parents in the program was that we would go to a Catholic school. I went there on scholarship.

When I walked through the doors of Bishop Moore for the first time I had no idea it would have a seminal influence on my life, so much so that I would maintain a lifelong connection with the school.

The first day you enter any school is always an adventure, but it helps to know the language. Not having full language skills, I felt a little alienated. The other students were friendly on the whole, though with the language barrier between us, they were not effusive. The Youngs made sure to emphasize that I should speak only English in school. Mrs. Young insisted, "Don't you Cuban boys go off in a corner and speak Spanish," adding, "The other kids will think you are talking about them and not like you." I tried to follow this advice as best I could, but I was also rescued from feeling isolated by the other Cuban kids at Bishop Moore, all of us now reunited after the camp. Naturally enough, we stayed together whenever we could, yammering away in Spanish and trying to help one another adjust and handle the schoolwork. The academics were certainly a challenge, given our limited knowledge of English. One thing I would definitely learn: Mrs. Young's advice about speaking English as much as possible, which at first I thought was too demanding, was *so* right.

Slowly I started to connect with the American kids. While the boys remained distant, the girls were friendly and started to reach out to us Cuban boys. Tricia Sagan was in my junior class and she took it upon herself to be a social worker, specializing in confused Cuban boys from Sagua la Grande. She came from a family of five girls that had taken on two of the "Cuban boys," as we were then known throughout the school and the community. She was very helpful and opened many doors for me and for other Cuban fellows in those first days.

Athletics were what helped me break the ice with some of the boys. I had always loved playing ball, any kind of ball, but I had only been aware of balls that were round—until Jimmy introduced me to football. He explained the game, and I sort of understood. Backyard touch football games appeared with the very few fall leaves in Central Florida. I even learned how to throw the football in a tight spiral. Over time, sports would continue to be an entrée for me in America.

Looking back, I see that through my first summer and fall in America, I was making some progress. I was hearing English spoken at home and at school 24/7, I was growing fond of the taste of peanut butter, I liked to throw a football around in games of touch, and in general I was starting to feel more like I was part of America, not just *in* America. Nevertheless, a great many adjustments still lay ahead.

❖   ❖   ❖

OFTENTIMES A big crisis is fueled by an accumulation of many smaller crises and frustrations. During my first year at Bishop Moore I received daily reminders that I was struggling to keep up with the other students academically and socially. I was a junior, taking classes with all the kids who spoke English as their first language. In class I would strain to translate as fast as I could, but my English vocabulary simply wasn't large enough at this point to grasp everything. I would work hard and catch key words. Sometimes I could comprehend enough words to reconstruct quickly what had probably been said. So I would move along partially comprehending what was happening. At night I could then study the text with the aid of a Spanish/English dictionary and try to keep pace with my teachers' instructions. But that didn't really work well enough. I was learning, but at a slow and insufficient rate.

This condition invites and then compounds frustration. Over the years I've spoken to many people who had learning disabilities, especially dyslexia, and they too suffered violent feelings of mental inadequacy out of all proportion to their slightly handicapped ability to learn. Their intelligence was fine, but the process of inputting the information was a little off-kilter. They were like cars with good engines but with clogged intake manifolds. That's the way I was. Back in Cuba I had been an average-to-good student. A photo of my sixth-grade graduation shows me carrying the Cuban flag, a special honor accorded to a good student who exemplified the values of good citizenship (though in my case it didn't hurt that I was also the tallest kid in the class). But suddenly in America I was

EASIER TIMES: My struggles to keep up academically in America were a far cry from my experience in Cuba, where I was chosen to carry the Cuban flag at my middle school graduation— something I was proud to do in those pre-Castro days.

having trouble with my studies, and it started to affect how I felt about myself.

I knew all these feelings stemmed from the language barrier. But still they persisted. At first I simply couldn't understand the teachers well enough. No one tutored me. Nobody. No one took me to night school for English, something I would do now with a kid in my position then. In those days schools offered no bilingual education, no psychological monitoring to help foreign students adjust. I was struggling and seriously discouraged.

The frustrations mounted. One time in history class the teacher announced we were going to have a "pop quiz." First off, I didn't know the term "pop quiz," let alone understand what it meant. I sat there befuddled. The teacher told us to take out a blank sheet of paper and to write our name on it. This I could follow and do. So in front of me on my desk sat a blank sheet of paper, just the same as the one that sat in front of all the other kids in the class. That's when the teacher lowered the boom: the pop quiz was oral. The teacher stood at the head of the class and spoke each question aloud. I couldn't understand a single word he said. If I had been able to read it and to have a little time to decipher it, I might have been able to do it. But the teacher made no allowance for that. I turned in a blank sheet of paper.

Chemistry class was even more daunting. I could never understand the teacher because he spoke as though he had marbles in his mouth. It was hard enough straining to make out the words from my other teachers and then quickly finding their Spanish translations to decipher what was being said, but with this mumbler it was impossible. I was completely lost in his class. Enduring such frustrations became more and more difficult.

That fall was when I hit a crisis. It all revolved around Homecoming Weekend. I didn't even know what Homecoming was. All I knew was that suddenly it was going to happen and the entire school was obsessed with it, the corridors abuzz about it every second between classes. Even though I was still woefully inadequate at English, I got the idea that this Homecoming thing was a very big deal indeed. Boys and girls were pairing off to go as couples, discussing what they'd wear, what parties they'd go to after the football game, and the dance that night. And there I was, out in the cold. I realized that I wouldn't be part of these festivities, wouldn't be going to the game or the dance or any of the parties. I didn't even know the particulars of what was going on. I only knew that it was the biggest weekend of the school year and I was missing out. I was just not like the rest of the students.

This realization hurt deeply. It heightened my feelings of alienation and isolation. Such a raw moment was also a painful reminder of how much I had depended on my father's counsel and my mother's tenderness, and how much I missed them now. This set off such a thunderstorm of negative feelings that I broke down crying.

My faith tells me to trust that God will provide someone or something just when you need it. In this time of need, Mrs. Young—Tía—came to me. She had been a total stranger to me only a few months earlier, and yet in this moment of my supreme isolation, she tenderly consoled me as my own mother would have done.

I was sitting in my room—Jimmy's old room, actually, God bless him—when I began crying. Tía overheard this and came in to talk to me, softly, kindly, maternally. She told me not to worry. She told me my feelings of being different and alone would pass. She told me I would soon be prattling away in English as fast as a tobacco auctioneer. Whatever you would say to someone to console them, whatever you would say to someone to make them feel better, Tía said it to me that night.

I remained pretty sad through the following days leading up to

Homecoming Weekend, but Tía had pulled me out of that deep well of depression into which I'd suddenly fallen. Tía's helping hand during this crisis allowed me to recall some wise counsel my father had given me—that tough situations would improve if I remained calm and clearheaded, if I reached deep down inside for courage and simply tried harder. He had told me that when faced with adversity I had two choices: either I could tell myself, "Okay, I'm going to wallow here and be a big baby and lose in life," or I could say, "Okay, I'm stuck here with a big challenge but I've got to keep trying, to get on with it, until I overcome it."

After that first crisis in America, which I weathered with Tía's incredible support, I became determined to get on with things, no matter how difficult the situation became. I told myself I *had* to get on with it. I wasn't just going to be pathetic here in America. Because I remembered my father's advice, I never entertained the idea of giving up.

But this forced me to realize something else about the challenges that lay ahead of me in America. As wise as my father's advice was, as much as he had tried to prepare me for the hard times I would face, the truth was that I could not rely on his counsel alone to get me through every crisis. After all, he had never lived in a foreign country, nor, while growing up, had he ever been separated from his parents and undergone the experience of living in a foster home. The grounding he had given me was powerful, but I intuited that from this point on, I was on my own. I was going to have to make it up as I went along.

Nov. 15, 1965

Queridos Papi y Mami:

Bueno Orlando se está vistiend de gala para la llegada de los Martinez-Ruiz.

Antes que nada quiero decirles que creo que tenga un trabajo medio lijado para Papi. El viernes pasado fui a ver a Mr. J.G. Lee el dueño de una lecheria aqui. Tiene dos fincas y mucho dinero. Bueno el Presidente de OJC. Mr. Hale me dio una carta de introducción y y asi fue la entrevista.

Yo - Bueno le expliqué que uds. no llegarían por un tiempo pero yo fui aconsejado de verlo a él pues el Dr. Eaton Volk me dijo (o le dijo a June.) que el tenia mucho ganado y nunca tenía veterinario pues todos estaban tan ocupado y que yo pensé que a lo mejor el tenia algo.

Me preguntó que edad tu tenias Papi.

Me pregunto: qué trabajo hizo el con animales grandes o chiquitos

Yo - grandes - ganado vacuno, equino y cerdos.

El - Le saber si el sabe inseminación artificial?

Yo - Si el ha hecho mucha inseminación artificial y el a nuevas tecnicas en esta rama.

LIFELINE: Fearing I would never see my parents again, I depended on our correspondence to sustain me. I wrote them long letters like this one every single weekend.

Chapter 6

CRISIS

EVERY TEENAGER IS taxed emotionally and psychologically by crises that later in life seem trivial. Sitting alone in my room on Homecoming Weekend at Bishop Moore, feeling left out, was just such an incident for me.

Without a doubt, the feelings this experience sparked in me, when I was just shy of my sixteenth birthday, were raw, powerful, and disturbing. But within a matter of weeks a far more significant crisis would put that experience in perspective, and radically accelerate my ascent to manhood. This was not a personal setback, but in fact a global crisis. It was the Cuban Missile Crisis.

And my family was at its epicenter.

To say this incident affected our lives would be an understatement.

❖   ❖   ❖

EVERYONE MY AGE can vividly reconstruct the tense days of October 1962 as the Cuban Missile Crisis unfolded. The churches were packed. Special masses were said, prayer vigils were held. There were exoduses from cities. People on the street showed fear and agitation in their faces. Everybody was tense. It was not uncommon to see people clutching rosaries and silently praying as they rode trains and buses.

None of this was an overreaction. Many years later historian Arthur Schlesinger Jr. described the Cuban Missile Crisis as "the most dangerous moment in human history." The Soviet Union had positioned nuclear missiles in Cuba and trained them on American cities like New York and Washington, D.C. Soviet commanders had been authorized to use the nuclear weapons if attacked by U.S. forces. Soviet leader Nikita Khrushchev was playing chicken with President John F. Kennedy.

As though it were yesterday I can recall every detail of sitting in the living room with the Youngs and watching the black-and-white TV. President Kennedy was speaking and I can still hear Tío say, "Well, this is it. This is World War Three."

After a moment of silence, Tía, in a voice scarcely above a whisper, replied, "My God, the world is going to end."

I sat there paralyzed. It was World War III and the theater of war was centered on Cuba. My homeland, the island paradise I had grown up in, was the battlefield. My parents, my little sister, my grandmothers, my whole extended family—they were all at ground zero for Armageddon.

❖   ❖   ❖

UNUSUAL PROBABLY FOR a fifteen-year-old, I remained glued to the television news reports, trying desperately to piece together what the English-speaking anchors were saying. I knew that what was happening in the news had massive personal implications for my family and me. The other kids in school understood this as well. As the confrontation between the United States and the Soviet

Union intensified, students asked me again and again, "What is going to happen in Cuba?"

I didn't know the answer, but I followed the crisis every step of the way: I saw the U.S. troop and armament trains rolling south down the length of Florida on their way to Key West; I saw the pictures of soldiers dug in behind machine-gun tripods on the Key West beaches; I stared at the televised images of U.S. warships forming the blockade of Cuba; I actually heard the fighter planes roaring overhead, flying in waves down to South Florida to be in strategic positions.

My parents, too, were eyewitnesses to the escalating crisis, as I would later discover. On the way to the dentist, my mother saw flatbed trucks driving through Sagua la Grande with huge tubes lashed to them and said, "What is this crazy man [Castro] doing? We are all going to die." It turns out the Soviets installed one of their missile battery sites right outside Sagua.

My sixteenth birthday fell in the midst of the crisis, on October 23. It was not a time for celebration. The day before, President Kennedy had given his first nationally televised speech on the crisis, revealing that the Soviets had nuclear missiles in Cuba and announcing the U.S. blockade. Then, two days after my birthday, I heard the U.S. ambassador to the United Nations, Adlai Stevenson, forcefully challenge the Soviets before the UN Security Council. When he demanded to know whether his Soviet counterpart really denied the missile sites in Cuba, he said that he would wait till hell froze over for a reply. In my still-broken English, I was unclear on the meaning of that expression, but I knew enough to understand that this didn't bode well for me or my family. It didn't bode well at all.

The parameters of the game had changed dramatically. I had

sense enough to realize that even if nuclear holocaust was somehow avoided, relations between the United States and Cuba would be far worse than they had been thus far in the Cold War. And that was why my family's plans would be shattered.

Through all my months in America I had felt confident that I'd soon be reunited with my family. Even when my father's three-month target passed, I knew that at least Ralph and Aunt Luisa had made it to America. My parents couldn't be far behind, I had told myself. But now, I knew, everything would change.

For the first time, I realized that I would be in for a long separation from my family. Maybe even a permanent separation. The hopes that had sustained me for months suddenly disappeared.

This whole nightmare scenario was totally real. I had to face the facts. My parents were stuck in a country ruled by a totalitarian Communist dictator. Meanwhile, my brother, just twelve years old, was living in difficult conditions down in Miami. As excited as I was that he had made it to America, I knew that he, Aunt Luisa, Uncle Mario, and their daughters were having a lot of trouble adjusting to their new circumstances. The language and cultural barriers, the lack of money, the cramped conditions with all of them in one small two-bedroom, one-bath house—this all made life for them hard. Ralph and I could keep in touch by mail and phone, but we were still more than two hundred miles apart. The only chances we had to connect came during school vacations, when I would catch a Greyhound bus down to Miami or he would do the same and visit me at the Youngs'.

Watching the Cuban Missile Crisis in real time, I was forced to confront hard realities: I might be on my own in this life indefinitely. My family's dislocation could last forever.

Forever. That word haunted me.

❖   ❖   ❖

IN THE END, the United States averted nuclear war. President Kennedy did not back off as the Soviets played their game of chicken, and he forced them to remove their missiles from Cuba in exchange for removing all American missiles from Turkey. But the secret Kennedy-Khrushchev pact that ended the missile crisis gave the Castro regime assurances that the United States would not take any steps to topple it. This promise put an end to any realistic opportunity for political change in Cuba. In the wake of the Bay of Pigs invasion, it was precisely what the dictator Castro needed to tighten his grip on power—and on the Cuban people.

Sure enough, Castro abruptly halted nearly all free travel in and out of Cuba. That included the Peter Pan program. I had been lucky to escape while I could. So had my brother, my aunt and uncle, and their daughters. But my parents and the rest of my family were stuck under Castro's repressive machine.

Only about a month after I fled Cuba, my parents had concluded that they were crazy to count on significant change for the good and that they, too, needed to escape to America. They began trying to get out of Cuba, but with all the paperwork and pre-travel restrictions involved, that process took a lot of time, as I had learned firsthand. Before their plans could advance very far, the missile crisis descended on them. In an instant, Castro had slammed the door. There would be no escape.

I was here and they were there. This divide, always painful, became almost unendurable, because it now seemed permanent. My only remaining outlet to family were letters and the occasional telephone call.

Our correspondence therefore became an important lifeline for me. In fact, my letter writing developed into a ritual. Every weekend, without fail, I would sit down and write my parents a long letter, covering everything from how I had done on a geography test, to a new friend I had made at school, to how life at the Youngs' house was, to how I had played in a basketball game.

My letters were, in other words, innocuous, chatty, and upbeat. That was by design; my family and I reflexively assumed that the Cuban government monitored our correspondence (and while we could never be sure, some letters might well have been censored). In my letters, and certainly in my phone calls, I never mentioned anything political, never criticized Castro's regime or spoke about the oppressive conditions in Cuba. My parents likewise avoided substantive issues. The political repression they endured was like the elephant in the room that didn't get talked about.

❖   ❖   ❖

As MUCH AS we avoided the topic, that repression was all too real. I received reminders of the cruelty of the Communist system from Ralph and Aunt Luisa after they fled to America. Some of them were deeply personal reminders.

Not long after I escaped Cuba, I learned, Castro's government had seized my uncle Rinaldo's dairy farm, the scene of so many wonderful memories from my childhood. The government official who carried out the confiscation was none other than Rinaldo's cousin.

The two cousins had been quite close; their grandfathers, the Cartaya brothers, had actually built this farm. But in Castro's totalitarian system, none of that mattered. In fact, the Castro government officials came and arrested Uncle Rinaldo and his wife, my mother's sister Yolanda. Yolanda was bedridden at the time, less than a week removed from a very difficult cesarean section to give birth to their second child. The Castro authorities pulled her out of bed at gunpoint and shoved her into the back of a jeep. She and Rinaldo were detained for the better part of a day before finally being released. In the ensuing months, my uncle would come down with rheumatoid arthritis. The disease could never be directly connected to this trauma, but it totally disabled him for the rest of his life.

Castro destroyed another place that had meant so much to me: my family's soda factory. As part of its attack on private ownership, the Castro regime decided that the privately held factory was too small. The government shut down the plant and dispersed the parts all over the country. So all of those who had worked for my grandfather for years and then for Uncle Mariano and my father—had worked at the factory, many of them, their entire lives—lost their jobs when the government "saved" them from the private-enterprise system. They went from supposedly being exploited to being unemployed.

This was life in Castro's "worker's paradise."

❖　❖　❖

WHEN I FINALLY acknowledged that I might never see my family again, it was, naturally, extraordinarily depressing. The experience of forced separation from my family was so searing it will stay with me forever.

This kind of separation is, of course, not uncommon in the American experience. After all, for more than two centuries people have been leaving behind family and homeland to come to America. The challenge, for me as for all the others who have endured such experiences, was to develop the skills to cope with the wrenching changes.

Looking back, I realize that the Cuban Missile Crisis and its aftermath toughened me beyond measure, made me reconcile myself to the difficulties of my situation. Just as I could not shrink from the reality that I might not see my family ever again, that I might never set foot in Cuba again, neither could I shrink from the responsibilities I had to my younger brother. Although I knew he had my aunt and uncle, I also understood that I had an additional duty to stand in for my absent parents from then on. A lack of money, the distance separating us, and our school calendars kept us from seeing each other often, but I made sure that we visited on school breaks.

I don't recommend this experience to anyone, especially someone who has just celebrated birthday number sixteen, but as a growth experience it was fairly unmatchable. It made me embrace self-reliance, that most American of virtues. I said to myself, once and for all, "This is it. I'm it. I don't have anyone to look to for help. I have to make it on my own and I have to do what I have to do." The whole ordeal made me who I am.

❖   ❖   ❖

I WOULDN'T FULLY comprehend the impact the experience of the Cuban Missile Crisis had on me until decades later, as I was writing this book. In the winter of 2007, I had my last conversation with Tía, Mrs. Young, as she was on her deathbed. I had one final visit with her, a leave-taking, a farewell. I told her again how much I appreciated all she had done for me.

As we were talking so affectionately, I brought up how she consoled me through Homecoming Weekend and then, hard on its heels, the catastrophe of the Cuban Missile Crisis. As I held her hand, I told her how much her advice, affection, and wise counsel helped to pull me through those agonizing experiences. I was so young then, I said.

She looked at me intently. "Yes," she said, "but you were always mature beyond your years, Mel. A few days after you were with us I said to my husband, 'Walter, this is not a boy anymore. He is already a man.'"

PLAY BALL: Baseball was king in Cuba, and it
would be a calling card for me in America.

Chapter 7

GRADUATION

WHEN THINGS HIT bottom they have only one place to go: up. Things started to improve after the missile crisis subsided and I got through that difficult first fall semester at Bishop Moore. Removed from the camps, I now experienced the exoticism of living in an American foster home, where I was immersed in the English language. I had started "getting around" a bit in English, as a tourist would, and by the beginning of the second semester, I could communicate in basic language, even if it was heavily accented and sometimes broken. My studies improved a tad, though my grades were still far lower than they had been in Cuba. Routine exchanges with the English-speaking kids started to happen with some frequency, and slowly I began to make friends with American students. Then a magic moment occurred as the late winter sun started to warm up the earth: baseball tryouts came.

My English teacher, Larry Mullan, also happened to be the baseball coach. Before class one day he pulled me aside and said, "Listen, why don't you go out for baseball? Come to the field after classes, and let's have a look at you on the ball field."

My heart jumped. *Baseball! Hallelujah!* This game had been my passion back in Cuba. Now I was being given a chance to rekindle my love for sports. I had missed the games I had played practically nonstop in Sagua la Grande. When I began at Bishop Moore I hadn't even been aware what high school football was, so there was no question of my going out for that. Basketball was a game I loved playing, but when tryouts had started in the late fall I was still struggling too much with English to pay any attention to them. So Mr. Mullan's invitation was a godsend.

On the appointed day I made my way to the baseball diamond behind Bishop Moore. For me it was the equivalent of a gem transported intact and unblemished from Cuba. It was just like the field behind my old school, Sagrado Corazón de Jesús. It had the same universal dimensions, the same brilliant geometrical layout. The feeling I had stepping on that diamond at Bishop Moore was like the feeling I had years later when I saw the film *Field of Dreams* and Ray Liotta as Shoeless Joe Jackson parted the cornstalks and walked onto that beautiful field in Iowa. It was that welcoming, reassuring, and familiar to me too. After so much time feeling like an outsider, I had found a place where I knew I belonged.

It didn't even matter much that when it came to equipment, I had zero, nada. Forget about bats, balls, and a glove; I didn't even have baseball cleats—just a pair of sneakers. As anyone who has played baseball knows, you are seriously handicapped without spiked shoes. Sure enough I slipped around on the grass and turf a bit, and couldn't dig into the batter's box to really drive the ball the way I had in Cuba. But I could deal with those frustrations. The other players were kind enough to lend me gloves, and I was just thrilled to be playing ball again.

I was excited, too, because baseball quickly became a way to fit in. On the field, language barriers suddenly don't matter much; when you hit a line drive everyone respects you. And let me tell you, I could really hit a baseball. Already six feet tall at age sixteen, I had a quick bat, good eye-hand coordination, and power. Playing ball was a way for me to break in, to be one of the guys, and not to be singled out as a kid who didn't know how to speak English. Hitting a baseball was just what I needed.

Unfortunately, a little heartbreak awaited me. Florida rules denied high school students athletic eligibility in their first year after moving into a new school district with a family not their own. The eligibility regulation was similar to the NCAA rule that requires a transferring player to sit out a year. It was designed to discourage kids from hopping around to schools solely on the basis of athletic considerations, and to prevent schools from stacking their teams with talent by loading up with kids from other school districts. I had hit the eligibility wall.

This reasonable restriction was a personal blow. Just when I had found something familiar to throw my heart and soul into, it too was taken away. It was as though my world crashed again. Sensing that I was devastated by this setback, Tía came to the rescue again. Nurturing and supportive, she counseled patience and stressed that I would get my chance next year.

She was right, so I decided to make the most of my year of ineligibility. Others tried to convince me that the eligibility rule was the result of prejudice, that it was meant to prevent Cuban kids from playing. But I listened to this with half an ear and dismissed it. The rule was for everyone, period. It had nothing to do with any racial, ethnic, or religious considerations. So I threw myself into the team, even if I couldn't wear the uniform and be on the roster. I became the student manager. I carried the duffel bag full of bats to games. I looked after uniforms and other equipment like pine tar for the batters and the rosin bag for the pitchers. I was the water boy and the scorekeeper. Whatever needed to be done, I did it.

Although I was not permitted to participate in games, I was free to practice with the team. This I did to the hilt. I caught batting practice. No one wants to catch batting practice. It's hard work, and it's hot crouching down with all that heavy gear on, but I loved it. Then, near the conclusion of each practice, I got my reward. I was allowed to step into the batter's box after all the other guys had taken their cuts. This sustained me. I lived for it. It opened people's eyes, too: soon people started to anticipate my hitting and would stay after practice to watch me drive the ball. People saw that I was a good baseball player and could help the team the next season.

Where once I had been completely lonely and bereft of my family and friends and all I'd known of life in Cuba, by the spring of 1963 my letters home had begun to be some fun to write. I was still distressed that my parents were stuck in Castro's Cuba and could not get out, but at least they weren't actively threatened with nuclear annihilation. Also, I could finally send them some cheerful news of my acclimation to school and my fun serving as student manager for the school baseball team. They were delighted to learn that in a year's time I would be eligible to wear the uniform of the Bishop Moore Hornets baseball team. That might seem trivial but it wasn't. It was emblematic of much more than simply baseball. Through the national pastime I was starting to connect with other Americans as an American. My parents sensed this and were cheered by it.

❖   ❖   ❖

SOMETIMES THERE WAS humor in this process of assimilation. One day after baseball practice I mentioned to Coach Mullan that I wouldn't be able to make practice the next day. I had a dental appointment, I explained. "I'm having two wisdom tooths pulled," I told him, simply adding an "s" to the noun as you would in Spanish. Ever the English teacher, he grinned at me. As the whole team walked the field toward the locker room, he blew the whistle and said, "Hey, fellas, Martinez is having two *tooths* pulled tomorrow." Everybody cracked up. But it was good-natured and I didn't mind, especially since Coach Mullan then took the time to explain the irregular plural "teeth." Believe me, I never made the same mistake again. Nor did I ever repeat the mistake I had made at school earlier that year when I said that in Cuba my father "married cows." That was my first attempt at explaining bovine artificial insemination.

But even though the kids would occasionally get a laugh at my English mistakes, I was coming along in my adopted language. Tía was a big help in this regard. Often I would come home from school and ask her to help me correct something I had said wrong that day. I would explain what I had said and she would teach me the right way to pronounce the word or to order the phrases and sentences. I picked up even more English that summer when I got a job working construction, where I hauled ceiling tiles for a building for Pan American Airways in Cocoa over on Florida's east coast. It's probably best to leave the phrases I learned from the construction workers unsaid.

In general, things were starting to come together for me, just as Tía had promised me they would. Not insignificantly, there was another development that spring that encouraged me a great deal and made me feel truly a part of the social scene: I got a girlfriend, a nice young woman I met in school. My letters to my folks began to mention her more and more.

❖　❖　❖

IT'S REMARKABLE THE difference a year can make. The transformation from my junior to my senior year at Bishop Moore was

EMBRACING AMERICAN LIFE: Outside the
Youngs' home in my school uniform
for Bishop Moore High School.

dramatic: I went from the lonely guy left out of the Homecoming hoedown my junior year to being on the Homecoming Court my senior year, along with my cheerleader girlfriend. The process of assimilation was now going full speed ahead.

Now eligible for all sports teams, in late fall I showed up at the gym for basketball tryouts. The coach was interested in me, for sure, since I'd grown to my full height of six feet two inches and put on some muscle as well. Right away he assigned me to the low post, what they now call the power forward. It was similar to the positions I had played in Cuba on our open-air court behind Sagrado Corazón de Jesús. Just as with the baseball diamond, the moment I set foot on the polished hardwood of the basketball court all was familiar. I was instantly at home there.

In fact, I was elected co-captain of the basketball team. I threw myself into the game, working tirelessly to contribute to the team with good hustle, solid defense, sure-handed rebounding, and occasional but unspectacular scoring. To my delight, my hard work paid off when I finally made it into the starting lineup two-thirds of the way into the season.

Through basketball I began to forge close friendships, some of which have endured right up to today. One of my good friends was Gary Preisser, the Big Man on Campus. Handsome, smart, and athletic, Gary was the star quarterback on the football team, a shortstop and starting pitcher on the baseball team, and the starting shooting guard on the basketball team. At six feet and about a hundred and seventy pounds, he had a perfect build in those days for a two-guard. Gary was responsible for the highlight of our season: a buzzer beater to defeat one of our principal rivals, Edgewater High, which was just down the street from Bishop Moore. Pandemonium broke out in the gym that night. It meant a lot to me that this BMOC would pal around with me, and the bond we formed has lasted for decades. Only recently I received a threat over my stance on a political issue. Who should call me up and offer his help? None other than my old teammate Gary Preisser.

Another close friend on the basketball team was Rick Steinke, who played center for us. Rick was taller than me, about six foot four or five, and played a solid center. Like Gary, Rick was terrifically helpful and generous to me. Both Rick and Gary gave me rides in their cars to practice, and we double-dated frequently. My date and I would pile into Rick's '54 Chevy or into Gary's '57 Ford with the right front fender missing, and off we would go to the Winter Park Drive-in to catch a movie. Sometimes we triple-dated. We would usually top off the evening by hitting the Steak 'n Shake for a snack. I'll never forget how Rick and Gary took this tall Cuban kid who spoke awkward, accented English under their wing.

I would have given anything to be with my parents during this time, certainly. I also regretted that Ralph and I were still apart, especially since I knew that he was in a more difficult situation than I was fortunate to be in at the Youngs' home. But without a doubt I had grown far more comfortable, and far less lonely, in Orlando. Forming close friendships, having a girlfriend, and knowing the Youngs well and feeling totally comfortable with them made a huge difference in my life. By now the Youngs were clearly my second family. All of us got a nice break when Mrs. Young's mother was able, with help from the money the family received from Catholic Charities for looking after me, to rent a small house a few blocks away. I went to live with her, and it relieved the crowding in the Youngs' home. It was pleasant to live with Mrs. Whalen, Mrs. Young's mother, in this cozy little house where we each had our own room. I had some much-appreciated increased independence under this new arrangement.

Settled and comfortable as I now was beginning to feel, history had a shock in store for me and for everyone else on the planet. One Friday afternoon basketball practice was abruptly halted and we were all sent home. In Dallas, President Kennedy had been assassinated. The shock of November 22, 1963, was like Pearl Harbor Day for an earlier generation and like 9/11 for a later one. We all remember where we were when we first heard the news. It was traumatic for the entire country, but for the Youngs it was especially so because they had moved to Florida from Massachusetts—in fact, they were Catholics from Massachusetts, just like Kennedy himself. They had suffered the loss of a hometown hero.

I came home from church that Sunday and experienced another disconcerting event. I was lounging around the house when I decided to turn on the TV and get the latest update on the Kennedy news. I watched as the federal marshals led Kennedy assassin Lee Harvey Oswald along a corridor, only to see a heavyset man step from the crowd with gun drawn and shoot Oswald to death. The marshals immediately apprehended the gunman. The scene was unbelievable, as though a fictional Western had come to life. Like millions of other people, I was dumbfounded. We were only a year removed from the Cuban Missile Crisis and it seemed as if the wheels were coming off reality again.

For me it was disconcerting that a Castro sympathizer had been Kennedy's killer. I wondered whether Castro was involved. My father would tell me years later where he was when he got the news of JFK's death. He was at a meeting in Havana with his employers at the National Institute of Agrarian Reform, the government agency that had taken control of every aspect of Cuban agriculture and therefore had become my father's only option for work. He vividly recalled going to this meeting and being told to return to Sagua because the United States would surely retaliate for the Kennedy assassination.

Four days later I passed the saddest Thanksgiving I can remember. The Youngs and I had the traditional Thanksgiving dinner with all the trimmings, but there was a heavy pall over the holiday. Everyone was still haunted by the TV images of the riderless horse with the boots turned backward in the stirrups and the catafalque rolling slowly down Constitution Avenue toward Arlington Cemetery. This was my first really strong impression of our nation's capital. Like many Americans, to this day I can visualize that scene and I can recall with sadness that solemn Thanksgiving. May we never pass such a somber holiday in this country again.

❖   ❖   ❖

AFTER THE ANGUISH of that late autumn, life, as ever, continued. By 1964 things were really starting to click for me at school—athletically, socially, and academically.

I had worked hard to improve at my studies. As my English progressed, my grades improved. They were still woefully short of where they would have been had I remained in Cuba and studied in my native language, but after feeling overwhelmed for so long I was delighted to begin grasping the language. That senior year I wrote, in partnership with a girl in class, an extensive paper on the contest that Senator Barry Goldwater eventually won for the Republican presidential nomination that year. This budding interest in politics was, I suppose, a legacy of being exiled and coming to this country seeking what now amounted to political asylum. It was also a natural outgrowth of being peppered by schoolmates with questions about the Cuban Missile Crisis in late 1962.

In Coach Mullan's English class we read Thornton Wilder's iconic American play *Our Town,* and I realized that Orlando was beginning to be *my* town—its places and people had become very familiar to me, and it had begun to feel a lot like home. I liked *Our*

Town for its attitude of altruistic concern for all members of one's community.

Years later Larry Mullan told an interviewer that he had admired the way I handled my class assignments from him, even when I didn't know enough subtleties in English to get the material straight. He told the interviewer that he respected my determination in always taking my studies seriously and handing in my assigned themes, essays, and book reports, even if I didn't always have my facts in order. I feel highly complimented by that remark, because I did try like crazy to make the grade. The compliment is even more special to me because Coach Mullan was, and remains, a shining example to me of commitment and service to others.

I got to appreciate his leadership even more that senior spring as baseball season began. Wearing the official Bishop Moore baseball uniform with the word "Hornets" scripted across the chest was a long-awaited thrill. I would no longer be simply smacking line drives into the power alleys after catching batting practice. I would be doing it in games, when it counted, hitting third in the order. Coach Mullan started me at catcher, first base, and even at third base for a few games. It was a tough season for our team—we managed only one win in eighteen games—but just being out on the field, after two years away from organized baseball, was an absolute joy. I was playing well, too. I still see Coach Mullan these days, and he sometimes laughs about the last game we played that year, when I hit three "screaming drives"—one that almost decapitated the first baseman, another that almost did the same to their third baseman, and a frozen rope off the bat that had the other team's pitcher ducking for cover.

Just as important to me were the friendships. Gary Preisser was again a teammate, and our bond only got tighter as we played baseball that spring. Then there was Tim Durkin, our starting second baseman. Tim gave me his hand-me-down cleats when he got a new pair. The old ones had holes in them, so we put newspaper inside to keep the dirt out of the sole. Yet the drawbacks and embarrassment of the hand-me-down gear didn't deter me; playing ball had always been too important to me. The experience did haunt me in a way, though: as a parent I would become fanatical about going to the sporting goods store and buying my kids new athletic shoes, cleats, or sneakers, even if the old ones only looked dirty.

I would also attend as many of my children's games as I possibly could, since the only sad part of my time playing ball at Bishop Moore was that my parents couldn't be there to root me on. All the parents would usually sit together in the bleachers. I would look to that area and just imagine that I could see my family there.

❖　　❖　　❖

A MAJOR MILESTONE came at the end of the spring: graduation. Only eighteen months earlier I had been forced to entertain the horrible thought that I might not make it to graduation because of the language barrier. The fear of flunking out had nearly paralyzed me. But now I was proud to be wearing a cap and gown in St. James Church (my home parish today) and walking across the altar to receive my diploma.

The only thing dampening my enthusiasm was the fact that I had no one there to celebrate with me. The Youngs were, rightly so, off at Jimmy's graduation from the nearby public high school. Ralph, Aunt Luisa, and Uncle Mario didn't have the money to make the long trip from Miami. And of course my parents were trapped in Cuba, refused permission to travel. My father, with his education and his veterinary knowledge, was considered an asset the newly restructured society could not afford to lose. I would have to celebrate this accomplishment with my buddies and my girlfriend.

After the graduation ceremony my girlfriend's aunt gave a little party at her house for several of us—Rick and Gary and their girlfriends, my Cuban friend Cesar Calvet and his girlfriend, and a few others. What made the event truly extraordinary was the hostess's gracious offer to me: she told me to use the phone to call my parents.

Remember, this was 1964, when making a long-distance phone call—*any* long-distance call, let alone one to Castro's Cuba—was a complicated and expensive procedure. When you phoned Cuba, the time spent waiting on the line for a connection could be interminable, and sometimes you just gave up in frustration and hung up. But that night I did get through. I was so thrilled to hear the joy in my parents' voices when I told them I had received my diploma. I don't know who was happier, my parents or me.

All those who have been separated forcefully from their families know the importance of such phone calls. The letters you send are fine, but they are no substitute for hearing the voices of your loved ones and knowing firsthand that they are safe and well. Of course, we knew as we spoke on the phone that the Cuban censors were eavesdropping, trolling for counterrevolutionary statements or whatever they imagined a seventeen-year-old with his newly minted high school diploma was plotting. At that moment it didn't matter. All of us reveled in this milestone and the sense of accomplishment that accompanied it.

What became a favorite adage of the Martinez family—practically a battle cry—ran through my head over and over: "Life goes on, life goes on."

CATHOLIC WELFARE BUREAU
CUBAN CHILDREN'S PROGRAM
1325 WEST FLAGLER STREET
MIAMI, FLORIDA 33135
FRANKLIN 7-8661

DEC 1 1965

November 26, 1965

Mr. Melquiades Martinez
c/o Catholic Charities Bureau, Inc.
132 E. Colonial Drive
Orlando, Florida

Dear Melquiades:

Now that you have reached your 19th birthday and have left the Catholic
Welfare Bureau Program, you are embarking upon a life which opens many
new challenges to you, and which I feel certain you are well prepared
to meet and conquer.

I realize well the difficulties you have experienced in being away from
your family, homeland, and all you hold dear.

It gives me pleasure that in some way the Church has helped you to bridge
the gap to a new life, making it easier for you to adjust to a new country which is most proud and happy to have received you.

I know well your desire to return soon to your homeland and your family.
I hope and pray that this happy event will not be long delayed.

It would be very helpful if you would keep this office informed of any
change of address so that we can continue to forward mail. I would also
like to hear from you from time to time to know what you are doing and
how you are getting along.

Asking God to bless you now and during the years which lie ahead, I am

Sincerely yours in Christ,

The Very Reverend Monsignor
Bryan O. Walsh
Executive Director

BOW/mjg

ON MY OWN: Once I turned nineteen I was no
longer officially under the care of the Peter Pan
program. Meanwhile, my parents and sister
were still trapped in Cuba.

Chapter 8

A NEW COURSE

L IFE INDEED WENT on that summer. But the key question was where it would take me.

I was entering a crucial transition phase but didn't know it. I was becoming accustomed to America, but inside I still felt Cuban. My parents were still living in our homeland and I still thought and dreamed in Spanish. Always in my mind was the key question of how—even whether—I could forge a reunion with my family.

In the short term, though, there were other questions, such as: What would I do after graduating from Bishop Moore?

I had hoped that my talents on the baseball field would earn me an athletic scholarship to either nearby Rollins College or St. Leo's College. Coach Mullan had even made efforts on my behalf. But neither school came through with an offer.

As much as I had wanted to play baseball on the collegiate level, that setback would not have been as much of a problem if I hadn't received a rather startling assessment of my academic future. This came from the guidance counselor at Bishop Moore.

I can still picture her very clearly in memory. She almost always wore her hair in a bun. When I expressed my hope to attend college, she fixed me with a serious look and said, "You really aren't college material. You ought to be an auto mechanic."

The worst part of this was that I feared she might be right, as would any vulnerable seventeen-year-old who'd just struggled through the last two years of high school in a foreign language.

Counterbalancing this horrible self-doubt was my father's firm conviction that I would attend college. He had always let me know that he assumed this was where I was headed, beginning as early as my first day of school, when I climbed on the bus in front of Grandmother Graciela's.

That made me set out to prove my guidance counselor wrong, but I nearly ended up proving her right. My first year of college I almost flunked out.

❖   ❖   ❖

THAT SUMMER OF 1964 following graduation from Bishop Moore, I worked two jobs. I was always hustling to make money, largely because I was desperate to try to get my parents and little sister out of Cuba. It was well known then that for a thousand dollars a head you could be smuggled out of Cuba via boat to Mexico. My brother, Ralph, and I were intent on raising the necessary three thousand dollars.

That was a great chunk of money back in those days. Hence my two jobs. One job was a part-time position working as a bag boy at Publix, the big supermarket chain. Putting on that white uniform always reminded me of my first day in America, when my cousin Manolito greeted me at the Miami airport in his Winn-Dixie uniform.

My other job, which had started on a part-time basis during my senior year and became full-time that summer, was at the Orlando Public Library, where I shelved books. At first I didn't give much thought to the library work. It was a job like any other. I certainly preferred it to the construction work I had done with Jimmy Young the previous summer, but I didn't like the falloff in pay. The library, a nonprofit organization, paid only ninety cents an hour. Even working full-time, I'd never come close to getting the money for my parents, not to mention what I needed to pay for school.

But the jobs provided other benefits. In Cuba I had done hard work helping out on my uncle's dairy farm and in my grandfather's soda factory, but I mainly did that for the fun of it and to spend time with family. Here in America I quickly learned to shoulder real jobs in order to survive economically. Working multiple jobs taught me strong lessons about economic realities and about handling money responsibly.

The library job, in particular, would have a significant impact on my academic career and my ultimate transition into American life. Quite simply, having to categorize and accurately shelve books required me to improve my English quickly. It helped that the books fascinated me. During downtime and on breaks I would crack open titles and start reading. Whenever I encountered words I didn't know I would look them up. Unlike the back, chest, leg, and arm muscles I had used in doing construction work, the principal muscle I was using here was my brain. My ability to read, write, and speak English benefited. I didn't quite realize it at the time, but this work was helping to prepare me for the intellectual challenges of college.

Those challenges were enormous. In the fall I started classes at Orlando Junior College, and the escalation from high school to collegiate academics was steep and daunting. Despite all the learn-ing I did at the library, my English still held me back in the class-room. My academic struggles would continue.

That first college semester hit me at a bad time. Mrs. Young's mother became ill, unfortunately, so she could no longer live alone in her rented house. This meant that I could not stay in that little house either. So we all packed back into Tío and Tía's small home.

The Youngs never failed to try to make me comfortable, but the truth was that there simply was not enough room for all of us. Since I had no car or driver's license, the crowded house was really my only place to study, and I struggled to find a quiet space where I could get work done. The bigger issue was that college academics were more rigorous than anything I had faced in high school, and I just wasn't ready.

The result was a terrible first semester. I especially struggled in English, a language I had just learned to speak and was still learning to write, and in science, a subject I had no background in. Things got so bad that I landed on academic probation. I thought I might flunk out of college almost before I had started.

Fortunately, one of the most challenging professors I encoun-tered also turned out to be a superb mentor. In my first semester at Orlando Junior College I took an English class with Dr. Rickert. He was a taskmaster with the reputation for being the meanest, tough-est teacher, brooking no nonsense and setting the bar high. Like any taskmaster he was a hard marker, and this only made students shy away from his classes all the more. I found out the hard way about his tough grading, but still, I loved what Dr. Rickert did within the four walls of his classroom.

To give you an idea of his approach, he would make students do countless vocabulary exercises. He had his own vocabulary lists that he had cobbled together over the years, and you had to commit each word on the lists to memory. You also had to memorize roots, prefixes, and suffixes. There was no faking it. You had to pore over those lists at night and get the information down pat to prepare for Dr. Rickert's tests. And, yes, those tests included "pop quizzes," which by now I knew how to handle.

My debt to this great teacher is incalculable. I realize what a catalyst he was in propelling my grasp of English to another level. Even today my mother-in-law, who is a stickler for good English usage, vocabulary, and grammar, will sometimes remark to me after she has seen me appear on television that my English is quite good for someone who didn't really start learning it until he was nearly sixteen. Each time she compliments me I say a silent thank-you to Dr. Rickert.

As my English improved, I met a second influential teacher and mentor. Professor Zimorski taught government and history. As with Dr. Rickert, I would end up taking multiple courses with Professor Zimorski and forming a close relationship that went beyond the classroom. Both Dr. Rickert and Professor Zimorski encouraged me and spent time with me.

Professor Zimorski and I would talk after class for hours about the international situation. Through him my already budding interest in world affairs blossomed into a passion, galvanized by the events in my life—revolution and a coup d'état, exile, separation from family, and the Cuban Missile Crisis. Geopolitics and government weren't just another academic assignment. I became intrigued by all of it: history, the Cold War, and the issues relating to my life experience with Communism. It extended to reading and discussing world events. I became a self-taught international observer. My passion for all of these areas of study was logical and organic: nothing had been more important to me personally and nothing had affected my life more.

◆ ◆ ◆

AT THE BEGINNING of January 1965, Tío and Tía recognized how much I was struggling to study in their overcrowded house, and they decided to see if they could find me a place where I could dedicate myself to school.

They approached June and Jim Berkmeyer, the couple who were supposed to have been my foster parents when I first left Camp St. John, to see if they could take me into their home. The Berkmeyers had an open space because my good friend Cesar Calvet had moved out when his parents arrived from Cuba. Sure enough, they agreed to take me in.

So at the beginning of my second semester in college I went to live with the Berkmeyers. Once again I was very lucky. It wasn't easy to leave the Young family, who had nurtured me through those agonizing days of 1962 and 1963. But the Berkmeyer home was perhaps the only place I could have felt comfortable moving to if I had to part ways with the Youngs. I had spent many nights at the Berkmeyers' while visiting Cesar, so I felt at home right from the start.

With a new living situation, and with the encouragement of Dr. Rickert and Professor Zimorski, I was able to buckle down to my schoolwork and began to excel in the classroom. Thanks to my academic turnaround, I was no longer assailed with self-doubt. I was even able to look back and chuckle at the Bishop Moore guidance counselor's recommendation that I become a Cuban-American Mr. Goodwrench. By now I knew that my father's determination that I attend college had been well founded.

Tía would later confess to me that while it was hard to see me move out of her house, she knew that at this stage in my life, living with the Berkmeyers would be good for me in many ways. The Berkmeyers were in a little better position to help me in the transition to adulthood. They understood the importance of my going to college and helped me achieve my educational goals as much as they could. Also, Mrs. Berkmeyer worked for the Florida Bankers Association and lived in a much more connected world than I had thus far moved in. Another reason they could really devote time and attention to helping me was that, unlike the Youngs, they did not have children of their own.

Some of the advantages were more prosaic, but no less significant to a teenager: I was now allowed to get a driver's license and borrow the family car on occasion.

Having the use of the family car once in a while made me less dependent on my buddy Rick Steinke, who also was attending Orlando Junior College. Still, Rick came through with lots of rides. He continued to pick me up for double dates on weekends, and during the week he'd give me a lift to and from school. Between riding to classes every day and going on double dates, Rick and I became almost inseparable. The two of us also spent a lot of time together on the basketball court. Rick played on the school's team, while, in a repeat of my early days with the Bishop Moore baseball team, I became a student manager. I kept in shape by working out with the team whenever my work schedule permitted.

That work schedule was the reason I hadn't tried out for the basketball team in the first place. I would have loved to play ball, but I had a pressing need for money—not just to try to rescue my parents from Cuba but, more immediately, to pay for school. By this point I had moved on from the library and the Publix in order to concentrate on a job with the YMCA, serving as an instructor and counselor to younger kids. Here I called on my experiences as an athlete—I coached the kids in flag football in the fall, basketball in the winter, and kickball in the spring—and as a Boy Scout, as I became a full-time instructor at the YMCA summer camp outside Orlando.

Life there at Camp Wewa even recalled my days at the beach house in Playa Uvero, since the camp was on a lake. I ended up teaching water sports to about a dozen ten-year-old kids and became certified as a lifeguard. Being a counselor and an instructor helped hone teaching and leadership skills I hadn't had an opportunity to use much yet.

I received other bonuses from the YMCA job. One was that the Optimist Club in Orlando noticed my work and in recognition gave me a small grant to help defray my junior college tuition expenses. Beyond that, being up at the summer camp gave me a welcome feeling of independence. As much as I loved living with the Youngs and then with the Berkmeyers, it was nice having my own space, even if I had to share it with a dozen loud youngsters. For once I wasn't a burden to anyone or an invader of anyone's space. I wasn't in anyone's way. It was great.

That summer I got to indulge another passion of mine: baseball. Though I hadn't gotten the baseball scholarship I had hoped for, that summer after my first year in college I still played competitively. On my day off from Camp Wewa I would ride into town and suit up to play American Legion ball for Post 242.

Baseball was always great fun for me, and I played the game well. To this day the overgrown kid in me still sometimes wishes that I had been able to give baseball a shot on the collegiate level. I was a good high school player, and every athlete wonders how far his talents might have taken him.

Some days, in fact, I will spot my Senate colleague Jim Bunning

Roots: Ralph and I were still separated by
more than two hundred miles, but we
visited each other whenever we could.

and think what might have been. As I kid in Cuba I saw the future Hall of Fame pitcher starring in the Cuban Winter League.

❖   ❖   ❖

ENTERING MY SECOND year of junior college, I felt more and more as if I was making a life in Orlando. Nevertheless, I made every effort to maintain my links to family and homeland.

When I went down to Miami during school breaks to visit Ralph and Aunt Luisa, it gave me a chance to reconnect with my roots, since I would see not only family but also old friends from Sagua now exiled too.

As always, though, my main priority was spending time with Ralph. I still felt that with my parents absent, he was my responsibility and we needed to have close contact with each other. Aunt Luisa provided him—and me—with emotional support, maternal care, and a strong tie to family at a difficult time, but the fact is that her household was full of the kind of turmoil brought on by the struggle to resettle in a new country.

Ralph was still only in his mid-teens, even younger than I was when I first came to America. After I entered college and began assuming a leadership role with the YMCA, I took my responsibilities to my younger brother even more seriously. I was his brother first, but I understood that in the tumult he was forced to endure at such a young age, I was also a surrogate father.

When Ralph would come to Orlando, I would do whatever I could for him. Sometimes I would buy him something nice, like a new shirt, or I would find something to do that he would enjoy, maybe the two of us taking in a movie or a ball game. More important, our time together in Orlando, just the two of us, gave us a chance to talk freely about our parents—how much we missed them and loved them, how much we hoped to be reunited with them.

All of our efforts, prayers, and hopes centered on finding a way to get them to America. In this regard there was a new rumor or scheme every month or two.

Invariably Ralph would invest too much hope in whatever the latest rumor or scheme promised. He would do this to the point of not moving on. He would get bogged down in it when it inevitably fell through.

I felt that I had to push him along whenever this happened. I didn't want to see him wallow in his disappointment and end up depressed and immobilized by the setback. When he stayed with me at the Berkmeyers' we would share a bed in my room and we'd have long talks, much as my father and I had done before I left Cuba. During these talks I would pass along some of Papi's wisdom, but I always felt inadequate to the task. I always believed that I could have or should have done more for Ralph, but I did what I could.

The best time we had in Orlando was Ralph's Christmas visit in 1965. I had told the Berkmeyers that what I wanted for Christmas was for them to invite Ralph to visit and to spend on him whatever they had planned to spend on me. He needed clothes and I was determined to help him get them. The Berkmeyers agreed. As it turned out, they still got me a sweater, but Ralph got a lot more clothing than that and had a terrific Christmas. Because of their good-heartedness the Berkmeyers wound up spending Christmas with a couple of pretty happy kids on loan.

The Peter Pan foster parents were a remarkable group of people. I have never ceased marveling at their generosity of heart and spirit. To answer a call for help from the pulpit on a Sunday morning and to follow through for years by caring for a foster child was magnificent. How easy it would have been not to have raised your hand, to have just let someone else do it. These foster parents chose to get involved and to give of themselves, and I have been forever grateful to them for what they did. They filled the role of parents when I was without my own.

❖   ❖   ❖

BY THE WINTER of 1966 I had spent four full years in America. The hopes of a quick reunion with our parents had, of course, long ago been dashed. I had endured dislocation, isolation, and the struggles of adapting to a foreign land with almost no support network. I had faced the frightening prospect that I might never see my parents again.

Confronting that painful possibility did not mean that I gave up hope. Together Ralph and I prayed for a reunion and did whatever was in our power to make it possible. For years we had only the sketchiest of information about what our parents were doing, since our parents rightfully feared alerting Fidel Castro's government to any plan for escape. Eventually, though, I saw how desperately my parents were struggling to flee when they abandoned their caution and began writing letters urging me to do certain tasks to help get them out. I knew the pain of separation I felt, but I could only imagine what it was like for my parents to be trying to extract themselves and their young daughter from Castro's Communist dictatorship.

It had been four years of waiting, and still we had no certainty that there would ever be a payoff. But then it happened—suddenly, magically, without warning. In the wee hours of a March morning in 1966, Ralph and I got the word: our parents were on their way to America.

Our long agonizing wait was over. The constant thought agitating us at the back of our minds would be stilled. The source of so many nightmares would disappear. The long and painful conversations with Ralph would now be rendered unnecessary. The overriding obsession in our lives was about to vanish with the materialization of our parents here in our midst in America.

THE MOMENT: After four agonizing years of
separation, my family and I were finally reunited.
Jim Berkmeyer captured this magical moment
on his home movie camera.

Chapter 9

REUNION

MR. GODWIN WOKE me up at about 1 A.M. My brother Ralph was on the phone, he said.

It was March 26, 1966, and I was in my cabin at Camp Wewa, where I was running a weekend YMCA group. Mr. Godwin, the camp caretaker, hustled me to his house so I could find out what was so urgent to require a phone call in the middle of the night. When we got there I saw that Ralph's call had awakened Mr. Godwin's entire family.

As soon as I grabbed the phone Ralph blurted out his news, scarcely able to control his excitement: *our parents were coming in two days!* He had just received word from our father via a phone call from Cuba, he shouted joyously. It had been a cryptic message, but one we both knew instantly how to interpret: "Violeta and Candelario are taking a very interesting flight on Monday." Violeta and Candelario were our mother's and father's middle names; "an interesting flight" could only mean that they were flying to Miami. Laughing, Ralph kept repeating these same words.

I was shocked at first that this moment I had anticipated for so long was apparently unfolding. I was afraid I still might be disappointed, but as the news sank in I was overjoyed and began to cry. My parents and our little sister were free at last. After more than four years they were coming to America to join Ralph and me, and our family would be a real family again. My stomach was leaping with excitement, my elation total. Mr. Godwin and his family understood the significance of this moment and they began jumping with joy for me. The Godwins, Ralph on the other end of the telephone line, and I—we were all exhilarated, shouting and cheering in those early-morning hours. I can still feel the chills running up and down my spine and the goose bumps on my arms.

For the next two days phone calls flew fast and furious back and forth between Ralph in Miami and me in Orlando. My extraordinary excitement was tempered slightly by the realization that with little money and no car, I couldn't get down to Miami to greet my parents at the airport. So I would stay put in Orlando, while Ralph, Aunt Luisa, and Uncle Mario went to meet our parents on the tarmac at Miami International. But through our flurry of phone calls we decided that our parents would come to Orlando as soon as they cleared customs and immigration in Miami. Aunt Luisa and Uncle Mario's small house was already overcrowded with Ralph living with them. Clearly Mami and Papi and our little sister, Margarita, could not move in with them. Plus, my father needed a job and I could help with that in Orlando.

I was the guiding force in bringing my family to Orlando. It would set a pattern that has endured to this day. Because my parents had lost their country, their heritage, and their language, I, from age nineteen, would parent them in America. In this strange and wonderful new country I knew the ropes and they didn't. In order to pull off this role reversal successfully I had to use delicate diplomacy, making sure never to usurp my dad's authority or to compromise his or my mother's dignity. Until my dad passed away in 1995 I managed to accomplish this, and I am still doing it to this day with my mom. It's a privilege.

This role reversal with parents was a universal experience for the kids in the Peter Pan program. By the time our parents arrived here, we were fluent in the language and had acclimated ourselves to the new culture and its customs. We were assimilated, even if we still spoke with accents, but our parents were alienated, knowing neither the language nor the culture. Many of us had to step up.

❖　　❖　　❖

IN MY MIND's eye I can still see the plane carrying my parents fly into Orlando Airport. In those pre–Disney World days Orlando's airport was only a small field with one medium-sized terminal building, nothing like the multiterminal international behemoth it is today. So I stood on the tarmac just outside the terminal door and watched the large prop from Miami on approach for its landing. I can still see the letters N-A-T-I-O-N-A-L emblazoned on the fuselage as it spun to a stop about fifty yards from me. There were no jetways back then either, so they rolled the portable staircase up to the side of the plane, the hatch opened, and the passengers started to descend. My heart was thumping, and my palms felt moist. What a sense of anticipation I had. Would my parents be strangers to me? Would I recognize my little sister, Margarita, who had been all of fourteen months old the last time I laid eyes on her?

With a huge lump in my throat I stared at the plane's open hatch. Suddenly I saw my mother step onto the small platform at the top of the rolling staircase and there, trailing her and holding her hand, was a pretty little girl of five clutching two dolls, one in the crook of each arm. Then my dad stepped into the open doorway.

By now I was waving frantically and my mother was waving back to me. I blew my mother a kiss, just as she had blown me a kiss at the Havana airport more than four years earlier. Her face lit up now and she was gesticulating to Margarita, urging her to wave to me.

My father stood there on the small platform for a second as my mother started to descend the staircase clutching Margarita's hand. That's when he tipped his hat to me. I waved back to him but I thought, "What is he doing with that hat on?" In Cuba my dad rarely wore a hat, usually only when he was in the country working, and yet here he was now climbing down the staircase with a big fedora like a gangster would wear. But I was reassured by his sunglasses. He always wore sunglasses back in Cuba. A few hours later when things had settled down I quietly asked him, "What's with the hat?" He looked at me sheepishly and said, "In the movies the Americans are always wearing hats, so I thought I had to wear one too." The fedora making him look like Humphrey Bogart was my father's equivalent to my drinking of cold milk. We both wanted to fit in right from the start in America.

When they reached the tarmac and started to walk toward the terminal I realized I had been frozen to the spot. Immediately I snapped out of it and started to walk toward them. I felt light-headed, giddy. This voice in my head said, "Is this really happening? Are they really here?" And just as quickly a voice in my head answered, "My parents are here. There are *my* parents."

As I neared them I felt the presence of the photographer from the *Orlando Sentinel* snapping away with his camera, and also of Jim Berkmeyer, who was tracking me with his home movie camera. When I reached my mom she grasped me in her arms, giving me a tremendous hug that I was overjoyed to return. I said a quick hello to Margarita, but she was shy with me at first. I finally looked up to meet my dad's gaze; smiling, he stepped forward and gave me a bear hug. After I hugged my parents I crouched down like a catcher and invited Margarita into my arms. She hesitated infinitesimally, then stepped into my embrace; that made four of us altogether in that embrace, since she still held the dolls.

By now my mother was dabbing her cheeks with a handkerchief, her eyes having overflowed with tears, but my dad just kept beaming and patting my arm. My mother hooked an arm around me and planted kiss after kiss on my face, her tears joining mine.

She looked from me to my dad and said, "He's not Melquiadito anymore. My little boy is a man now, bigger than you." It was true. I had a good three inches on my dad. I was no longer "Little Melquiades"—in more ways than one, as I was soon to learn. My mother kept sculpting my face with her hands and asked, out of the blue it seemed to me, whether I had undergone plastic surgery. Of course I hadn't, but my face at nineteen had shed the baby fat she had known and had acquired the sharp jawline and chiseled features of young manhood.

After we had collected the little luggage my parents had, we loaded ourselves into the Berkmeyers' car and started the drive to their house. The Berkmeyers, bless their hearts, had solved a huge problem for the Martinez family: they had invited my parents and my little sister to move in with us until they could make other arrangements. So we were reunited under one roof, all except for poor Ralph, who stayed down in Miami because our parents would not uproot him from school with only two months left to complete the term. Ralph would stay in Miami with Aunt Luisa and Uncle Mario until he finished his classes and then would join us in Orlando.

I will never get over the feeling of unreality that came over me as I sat wedged between my parents in the backseat of the Berkmeyers' car. We were zipping along 15A in the direction of the Rio Pinar neighborhood, and all I kept thinking was: "The two people sitting next to me are my actual mom and dad." I swiveled my head from side to side, glancing at each one in turn and saying to myself, "Yes, Mel, this is really happening. You are not dreaming. This is it. This is real. This is them, your natural mom and dad. They are truly here. It's all *real*."

I felt tears welling in my eyes and put my head back for a second. When I leaned forward again, there it was on an overhanging directional sign, that English word I had puzzled over the first night I arrived in America: AHEAD. Only now I knew what it meant. I wondered what the future held for all the Martinezes.

❖   ❖   ❖

Now I FINALLY learned the details of my parents' long struggle to escape Cuba. When, in October 1962, Castro halted flights to America in response to the Cuban Missile Crisis, it was just the first missed opportunity my parents had to endure. They had always held out hope that Cuba's government would be overthrown, but the Cuban Missile Crisis convinced them once and for all that they too had to get out—except now they *couldn't*.

There seemed to be a possibility when, in 1965, President Lyndon Johnson and Castro reached an accord that provided "Freedom Flights" to allow Cuban parents to reunite with the fourteen thousand Peter Pan kids in America. Unfortunately, the frustrations continued for my parents even then. Once my father was forced to go to work for the National Institute of Agrarian Reform, known as the INRA, it became even tougher for my parents to get out of Cuba. This agricultural ministry valued my father's skills as a trained and experienced veterinarian, and the Communist regime, fearing a "brain drain," wanted to retain and exploit as many educated professionals as possible, including my father. That made it nearly impossible for my parents to get clearance from the government to leave as part of the Freedom Flights.

What accounted for the miracle of their escape was a story that sounds like a subplot from *Casablanca.* In doing some work for the INRA, my dad formed a friendship with a Cuban army colonel who was also a veterinarian. This colonel took pity on my dad and my mom for being trapped in Cuba with their toddler daughter while their two teenaged sons were in America, effectively orphaned. It so happened that the colonel was having an affair with a woman whose sister was having an affair with the head of immigration, and he prevailed on the immigration official to help my father leave Cuba. Pulling off the plan required all kinds of cloak-and-dagger intrigues. The colonel used to coast up to our house late at night in his big car with the headlights off to avoid detection. Then he would sneak into the house so he could discuss, in a whisper, the plans to get my father out.

Finally, they arranged to have my parents leave on a day when most of the high-ranking government officials would be away at the beach. A sergeant from the Cuban army came to our house and stripped it of anything valuable, then gave my dad a false affidavit to sign, listing only cheap items. The sergeant had earmarked the truly valuable possessions for sale on the black market and, who knows, maybe even for a kickback to the savior colonel. This was the kind of corruption that reigned in Cuba's Communist government.

Even with all the elaborate preparation, my dad almost didn't make it out of the Havana airport. When he stepped forward to board the plane, a Cuban soldier refused him clearance because his name was misspelled on the passenger manifest. My dad had to step back out of line. But there was an official from the U.S. State Department monitoring the whole process. He coolly fished a full pack of Chesterfields from his pocket and handed them to the Cuban soldier. While the soldier was distracted by his good fortune in receiving the cigarettes, the State Department official corrected the spelling of my dad's name on the manifest and nodded for him to go through. Stunned, my father hesitated a second, then shot through the gate. With my mother and Margarita in tow, he boarded the Mackey Airlines flight bound for Miami.

About forty-five minutes later, at 11:30 A.M., the plane landed in Miami International. Ralph loves to tell the story of how he met their plane, which landed way off to the side, away from the main terminal. Ralph stood on a rooftop deck at the terminal, and when he spotted our parents deplaning he waved and hollered. But they looked at him without recognition, thinking he was a friend or family member of the *other* Cuban exile who stood next to him, waving excitedly at relatives of his own on that flight. Finally, our mother turned to our father as they walked across the tarmac and said, "You know, I think that kid up there is Ralph."

"Woman," our father replied, looking directly at his younger son, "don't be silly."

A few paces later they could hear Ralph, and our dad knew instantly that a woman's intuition had triumphed yet again. Of course, Ralph had changed a lot in four years too. He was almost sixteen now, and vastly grown up compared to the twelve-year-old they had said farewell to back in June 1962.

Within minutes of their clearing customs Ralph was able to share an emotional reunion with our mom and dad and little Margarita. But his reunion with Papi was cut abruptly short when the CIA took our dad away for a debriefing. U.S. intelligence wanted to know as much as he could tell them about the Russian missiles that had been positioned in Sagua. Papi was able to tell them such details as being able to set his watch by the U-2 reconnaissance overflight every noontime. Ralph went home to Aunt Luisa's small apartment that afternoon with Mami and Margarita, but the CIA didn't drop off our dad until the next day.

❖   ❖   ❖

PART OF WHAT lured my parents to Orlando was work: I had lined up a job for my dad.

Whenever I had visited Ralph and Aunt Luisa and Uncle Mario, I had seen that my aunt and uncle tended to be depressed about their prospects in America. That was understandable. After all, it is hard enough to find work as an architect even when you have a full command of the native language. It is infinitely harder when you have to communicate in a new language in a foreign country. Uncle Mario was having a tough time of it, and so when we found out about the Freedom Flights out of Cuba and thought my parents might be getting out, he and Aunt Luisa naturally thought the same fate would befall my dad in America. But I didn't want to accept that.

When I mentioned my concern to June Berkmeyer, she called her veterinarian, Dr. Caton. Unlike my dad, he mostly handled small animals, and I thought my father might end up cleaning dog kennels and cat cages. But it so happened that Dr. Caton was the veterinarian for the T. G. Lee Dairy in Orlando, which had a herd of 2,000 cows. Since my father was a large-animal vet who had ministered to herds and herds of cattle in Cuba, Dr. Caton thought T. G. Lee could be a good fit and said he would make an inquiry on behalf of my dad.

Dr. Caton kindly set up a meeting for me with Mr. Lee, the head of his family dairy. I put on a coat and tie and went, with some trepidation, to see Mr. Lee. A receptionist walked me through a fairly large office crammed with desks positioned every which way and alive with the sounds of typewriters clacking and phones ringing. At the back of this large room was a door leading to a smaller room set into a corner. This was Mr. Lee's office. He was a kindly older man with thick glasses and a ready and welcoming smile, an easygoing manner, and, in the midst of the Cold War, a serious dislike for Communism. This we shared. It was evident to me as I sat in his office chatting with him that he wanted to help. I will always recall the warmth in his big blue eyes behind thick glasses. I left there with my feet hardly touching the ground. Mr. Lee concluded our talk by telling me that my father should call when he got to Orlando.

So upon my father's arrival, I called Mr. Lee and arranged for my father to interview with the farm manager, Mr. Robinson. At that point, everything nearly went off the rails. My dad had serious trouble communicating with Mr. Robinson, since he knew only a handful of English words and phrases. He struggled to communicate his knowledge of cows and how to minister to their needs. My spirits were sinking when Mr. Robinson suggested we visit the farm's animal pharmacy. This was like a sunburst after a heavy thunderstorm. The minute my dad stepped into the room and saw the shelves upon shelves of pills and serums and bandages and needles and dressings, he lit up. In Spanish or English—or for that matter in any language—the names of the medicines are the same.

Papi started rattling on. I translated. Mr. Robinson grinned and began firing questions for my father at me in English. On the spot I became a simultaneous translator. My dad shot back each answer, dead accurate, in Spanish. Talk about faith in action and the hidden hand of God at play: not only did my dad win himself a job, but I stumbled on a talent, simultaneous translating, that would ultimately help lead to my vocation in life, public service.

❖   ❖   ❖

MY FAMILY WAS thrilled to be back together, and thrilled that my father had found work so quickly. Of course, we were also confronted with practical and logistical challenges, and it was up to me to meet them. To get Papi to work, first we had to get a car. I had managed through my various part-time jobs to save enough money,

$250, to buy a used Chevy, a gray '59 Bel Air, with the big horizontal fins in back. This Chevy was only slightly newer than the old scoop back we used to coax out of the mud in Cuba. Since we had only the one car and I needed it all day—to go to class, to drive my sister to school, and to get to my part-time job—I was up like a farmer every morning to drive my father to the dairy.

First my dad would get up and go through his morning ritual of having breakfast and dressing for work. My mother would be up with him. When he was ready to leave for the dairy my mother would wake me up, but not an instant sooner, since she wanted me to get all the rest I could. Many nights I would stay up late studying or be out with friends, and this was one early call to reveille, believe me. I would stagger out of bed, pull on my pants, splash water on my face, and then run out of the house. My dad would be sitting in the car, nervously glancing at his watch and drumming his fingers if I was even a tiny bit tardy. He was a man to honor rules, and one of the principal rules was never to be late for work. I'll tell you how serious he was about this matter of following the rules: after we bought the Chevy and parked it in front of the house, my father would not allow it to be driven until it was insured. So he and I walked about a mile and a half, maybe two full miles, to the insurance office to buy the insurance. Then we walked the same distance back home. It makes me smile now to think of it, but it was a great example to set.

Another role reversal occurred when I took my dad for his driving test. He was so nervous that his left foot kept shaking and he had trouble controlling the clutch. I sat in the backseat translating for my dad and the examiner, but I made sure to slip in a few words of encouragement for my father while I translated.

As soon as my dad got his driver's license, he would drive to the dairy while I dozed off in the passenger seat or chatted with him. When we got there he would wake me if I was asleep and hop out. I would then drive back to the house and get myself ready for the day. I would take my little sister to school first, then drive myself over to Orlando Junior College and attend classes. In the afternoon I would reverse the process. I'd retrieve Margarita at school, go to my part-time job, pick up my dad at work, and bring us all home for dinner.

That daily routine was never easy to pull off, but dinner was always a pleasure. Even while we lived with the Berkmeyers a routine developed whereby my mother would fix the evening meal. June would have been out at work all day, and besides the bonus of not having to come home and prepare a meal, she and Jim loved the steady diet of good Cuban cooking my mother served up. I of course loved it even more. I loved readjusting to Cuban food on a regular basis. After dinner, all of us would talk on into the evening, filling in the gaps of all that had happened in the past four years of our separation and making plans to cope with the challenges ahead: finding housing and working out a budget and many other details of re-settling in a new environment.

One evening after everyone else had gone to bed, June and I stayed up late talking. After a while she started to cry. She said it had become obvious to her that I would be leaving to live with my parents. This came as a crushing realization for her. She cried and laughed at herself for having thought that somehow I would remain living with her and Jim. But of course she was gracious and under-stood that I had to leave, and even that it was my good fortune to finally be reunited with my family. Eventually we both went to bed a little sad and a little glad. As with Mrs. Young, so with Mrs. Berk-meyer: we would remain as mother and son until her death years later, when Cesar and I sat in the surgical waiting room refusing to accept that June would shortly be gone from our lives forever.

My bond with the Youngs and the Berkmeyers lasted a lifetime. I had three sets of parents. Mother's Day was fun; in fact, it was triple the fun, buying three cards and gifts instead of just one. With these two outstandingly generous families I shared a lifetime's worth of good times and bad times. I am still in touch with both Young boys today, Jimmy and Dennis, and it was a grace note in my life that I was able to eulogize Tía and Tío at their funerals, just as I also eulogized June at hers. In between sobs, with a mixture of warm and humorous memories, I said farewell to them in fine style. It amused and pleased me that they would have pointed out proudly that a United States senator had eulogized them. I would always grin and be grateful to God every time it would get back to me from friends and acquaintances that they had referred to me as "my foster son, the senator." According to my sources, Tía used to add, "When you help someone, you never know what will come of it." They were glorious.

❖   ❖   ❖

MY MOTHER, FATHER, sister, and I lived with the Berkmeyers for three weeks in that spring of 1966. Then, good fortune struck again when Jim Berkmeyer, who was a Realtor, found a modest house for us to rent. The house, at 2822 East Pine Street in Orlando, had three small bedrooms—one for my parents, one for Margarita, and one for Ralph and me to share when he moved up to Orlando at the end of his school term down in Miami. We could meet the rent with my dad's salary, my part-time earnings, and the money my mother brought in through occasional hairdressing jobs. In Cuba, the money she had earned as a hairdresser had been a nice bonus for the family; now it was needed. My mom would work terrifically hard for many years in America, capitalizing on this skill she had learned in Cuba in order to help the family.

As we settled in to our new home and new life, I showed my parents a lot of the basics they'd need to know. My dad had only his slight grasp of English and my mom knew next to none, so I was the interpreter. One skill I showed them was how to shop at an American supermarket. Another was how to manage our money. At first my father insisted on paying for everything with cash. That meant I found myself driving our old Chevy to the utilities company to pay the bill, then to the phone company to pay the bill, then to the Realtor's to pay the rent—everything paid for in cash. Finally, after two or three months of this, I had to put my foot down and insist he open a checking account. He protested, saying he had no money. He wasn't sure he could open an account, thinking the bank would need to extend him credit to do so. I explained to him that a checking account involved no credit. It was not a loan. I told him that if he put his paycheck in the bank he could draw on it with personal checks as long as he kept a sufficient balance on hand, just as he had done with his business account in Cuba. Finally I convinced him, and we began to pay our bills by mail like everyone else in America.

My dad soon grew to like having the convenience of a checking account. He liked becoming an American. A short while later he and my mom began taking English lessons at night. I drove them to the First Presbyterian Church downtown for their English as a Second Language classes. My dad started to pick up English fast, especially because he had to use it every day at work. My mom was different. She was isolated most of the day at home, speaking to Ralph and Margarita in Spanish. She made some progress with English, but then, unfortunately, she just kind of stalled. My dad pushed himself to keep improving and wound up fluent in English, even if it was sometimes halting, always heavily accented English. He was proud of this accomplishment. He loved to talk so much that he just had to learn.

The environment at work certainly helped him achieve this goal.

When I picked up my father at the dairy at the end of the workday, Mr. Robinson would huddle with him and me to discuss the little things that the two of them had had trouble communicating about. For example, Mr. Robinson would check his notes and say to me, "Ask your dad, when we worked today in that pasture in the back, what was the problem with the calf he was trying to tell me about?" I would translate this into Spanish for my dad. He would explain what was wrong with the calf in detail, and I would relay this response in English to Mr. Robinson. By clearing up whatever communication gaps had come up, they would be fully oriented with each other when they resumed work the next day. During this ritual my dad would listen intently to my English answers and on the car ride home he would review the responses with me, memorizing them and working on his pronunciation. After a time he and Mr. Robinson were able to communicate with each other very well.

As pleased as I was to see my father's progress, I knew the transition to America was difficult and I wanted to be sure I was there to help my family. In the fall of 1966 I could have gone off to Florida State University in Tallahassee, where both my buddy Rick and I were accepted, but I deferred my acceptance for another term. So while Rick went to FSU, I stayed in Orlando. Fortunately, I still had a few credits I wanted to acquire at the junior college.

That fall the Orlando community came through for me yet again. I went back into my school's placement office looking for a job, just as I had when I got the great position at the YMCA. It turned out that Rutland's, the local fine men's clothing store in downtown Orlando, was looking for a salesman for its shoe department. I got lucky and got the job. I was fortunate to work in retail sales because it entailed direct contact with the public. That taught me a lesson every day. I had always been a people person, but the job helped me develop my interpersonal skills and gain insights into others.

I was fortunate in another respect too. Rutland's was the kind of store I would have window-shopped only, taking a wistful look at the top-shelf clothing on display before hurrying on down the street to J. C. Penney. But when I received an employee's discount I started getting really good clothes and shoes at affordable prices. Not only that but I learned *how* to dress. Naturally, the owner, a gifted and generous man for whom the store was named, Mr. Joe Rutland, wanted his sales personnel to look their best and thereby showcase his inventory. So every Saturday morning before the doors opened, he gathered the staff for short seminars on how to handle yourself, how to dress, and what was happening in the fashion business. He told us how he wanted us to look and act in the store at all times. We never removed our suit coats, loosened our ties, or indulged in any chitchat when customers were present. These mini-lectures taught me a lot about how to look like a gentleman and leave a positive impression on people.

After I graduated from Orlando Junior College in January 1967, I worked full-time for Rutland's for three months before the spring quarter at FSU began. The extra money I made gave me a chance to save for my upcoming college days in Tallahassee.

In those last months before my time at FSU started, I made sure to show my parents everything I could about life in America. One particularly humorous incident occurred right before I left. I took my mother and father to the Laundromat to teach them how to use the machines. Two women watching us, who did not understand our conversation in Spanish, assumed that my parents were instructing me on how to use the machines. I was obviously college age, so it made sense. But no, it was the other way around. It was another case of the child being the parent. I was in that familiar role of the Peter Pan child.

Of course, I still felt responsible for my parents and experienced some apprehension about leaving them and going to Tallahassee, which was 250 miles away. But it was clearly time for me to go. After all, it was my father's lifelong ambition for me to graduate from college. Besides, my family had made great strides, especially my father, whose English had come a long way by now. I also knew that Ralph, who had been with them for almost a year, was ready to take the baton from me. He was now sixteen, he spoke English as well as I did, and he had just learned to drive. He'd be driving a different car, though: my parents insisted that I take the Chevy with me to school. They got an even worse car. They adamantly pointed out that the Chevy had been bought with my money and that I would need the nicer car to make the long drive between Orlando and Tallahassee.

I'm happy to report that when I left them everything worked out okay. Ralph picked up the slack, helping them out at home and explaining the customs of the new culture. They also had a number of Cuban families nearby they had befriended, including some they had known distantly back in Cuba. This meant they had a community to fall back on and socialize within. They would attend the Spanish mass at six o'clock at St. James Church. So my family was doing just fine when I drove away from the curb in front of that little house on Pine Street in April 1967, headed for my first taste of life at a big four-year college.

My next six years in Tallahassee were going to enrich my life in so many ways that it's incredible for me to contemplate even today.

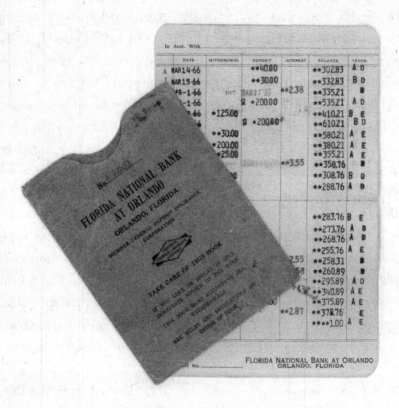

New beginnings: Working hard and slowly
saving money, my family and I put
down roots in America.

Chapter 10

OWNERSHIP

I N TALLAHASSEE A whole new world opened for me. Everyone who goes away to college experiences the exhilaration of feeling like an independent adult for the first time. For me it was a little different. I had experienced that feeling of being on my own five years earlier, when I landed in Miami as a fifteen-year-old without any family. But with that came not exhilaration but isolation. Even as I adjusted to being apart from my family, I always felt as if I was imposing myself on others, despite how gracious and welcoming my two foster families were. Now, in Tallahassee, I was no longer a burden on others. I was even free of the rules and regulations of a college dormitory, since I took a place in a small house with my high school buddy Rick Steinke and another Bishop Moore grad, Jim Necrasson.

I was fortunate to live with Rick, since he had already been in Tallahassee a few months and could show me around. Rick, Jim, and I had a good time living in that house together. Friends always dropped in to enjoy the good meals that Jim cooked, and the three of us went out for dinners or the occasional beer together. It was a fun and exciting time, and I really took to life in Tallahassee. It certainly was a vibrant atmosphere. After World War II, the state had expanded what had been the Florida State College for Women in order to accommodate returning servicemen and servicewomen who wanted to pursue higher education through the GI Bill. The state made the school coed and renamed it Florida State University. When I went there, the law school had just started and many other programs were beginning to flourish. Athletics were taking off as well; in my time as a student I was active in intramural sports and developed a lifetime love for the intercollegiate teams fielded by the FSU Seminoles. Despite the rapid growth, the university's student body was still majority female back then. That also made Tallahassee an exciting environment! Every weekend, caravans of male undergrads from surrounding colleges, and even from as far away as the University of Florida in Gainesville, poured into town.

As much fun as I had in Tallahassee, I was pretty busy with school and with the job I got almost as soon as I had registered for classes. I owed the job to Rick. He worked for the student newspaper, the *Florida Flambeau,* canvassing for ads on a commission basis, and he quickly got me hired in the same capacity. The money I earned covered my rent and gave me a bit of pocket change. But more important, it made my education possible; I needed to come up with tuition money since I could not count on financial help from my parents, who were just getting by back home. This job also gave me my first taste of entrepreneurship: what I earned depended on what I did. It wasn't like working for wages as a laborer, bag boy, library assistant, or YMCA camp counselor; even working at Rutland's, where I had earned a small commission on each sale, I had drawn a base salary. This newspaper job was pure capitalism, with all compensation pegged to sales. Sink or swim, all or nothing. I loved it.

I also did pretty well at it. I regularly made the rounds to the stores, restaurants, and shops in town and tried to convince them to take ads in our paper. I had a core of advertisers I called on, making certain they were happy with the result of their latest ad while also renewing their advertising commitment and encouraging them to upgrade it. I always tried to expand my customer base as well, so every round I'd make at least one or two calls on businesses that were not yet customers. This was only prudent if I wanted to maintain my income and the newspaper's revenue, since a regular customer would occasionally have to cancel an advertising commitment.

The financial incentives were not the only thing I liked about the sales job. Even better, I could set my own hours, soliciting the ads whenever I wasn't in class or studying. Flexible hours were ideal. There was no time clock and I was my own boss. It was the first self-starter kind of job I ever had. The more I worked, the more I made. It was terrific to have that kind of workplace responsibility, to be on my own recognizance. Having the Chevy certainly came in handy, since it allowed me to get to establishments in outlying towns as well as within Tallahassee proper. The work all paid off, too, as I typically netted about a hundred dollars a month, which was good for that time. Before I got to Tallahassee I hadn't known exactly how I'd support myself and pay for school, but this was the perfect opportunity for me.

Overall, life in Tallahassee was good. The language barrier was long gone, and I had friends, a car, a job, and intellectual interests. This was a good time for me and about as normal a life as I had experienced since I arrived in the States.

❖   ❖   ❖

WHAT MADE THINGS at school even better for me was that back home things were going well too. My family back in Orlando was never far from my mind. Every Sunday night, religiously, I called them on the phone for a long chat, since I couldn't be present for our big family dinner. These Sunday dinners were a ritual in our family. (In fact, they still are; to this day my brother Ralph and I go to our mother's house every Sunday night with our families, as long as we're not away on business.) From these weekly calls I learned that Ralph had stepped up to his new responsibilities beautifully. He was helping our parents, even serving as their live-in simultaneous translator, just as I had. This was a major relief for me in Tallahassee. It freed me to concentrate on my education.

My parents were taking to life in America, but things were never easy for them. They were spending nearly half their monthly income on rent, like most immigrants, not the financially "prudent" and universally recommended one week's income. So by the time they paid the rent, bought clothes and food for themselves and Ralph and Margarita, and covered utilities, there was no money left. In fact, there was not enough money left to send Ralph to Bishop Moore, something that always caused me a bit of chagrin. I had been privileged to attend Bishop Moore only through the help of the Peter Pan program and my continuing educational stipend from Catholic Charities. Ralph was not lucky enough to be under the same arrangement, so he had to attend the public school, Boone High School. But Ralph loved Boone and did very well there.

My parents had no money for furnishing their rented house on Pine Street. What furnishings they had were supplied through the generosity of friends and strangers. That generosity is a big part of why I love Americans so much, Floridians especially, and Orlandians inexpressibly. Mr. Lee, the head of the dairy where my father worked, called my dad into his office one day and told him to go over to a house with one of the firm's trucks and take anything he needed, absolutely anything. Mr. Lee was putting the house up for sale because he and his extended family no longer needed it, but he was so generous that he thought to take care of my family before he did anything. Furniture, appliances, pots, pans, utensils—my dad discovered plenty to outfit our house on Pine Street very nicely. Mr. Lee was magnificent to my family. Even now I have Mr. Lee's waffle iron; it still works. Ralph laughs when he recalls the beautiful four-poster burl-wood bed that Mr. Lee gave us. Its posts were large for the tiny bedroom, of course, and my mom, not aware that it was on its way to being a precious antique, showed it to a Cuban friend in the parish who happened to be a carpenter. You guessed it: he cut off the posts.

My parents this entire time in Orlando were extremely cautious financially. My father was paid every Wednesday afternoon, and by every Wednesday morning the previous week's pay had all been spent and we were effectively broke until he got his new paycheck. Every Wednesday evening after he received this latest paycheck, we drove to the Cash and Carry on the outskirts of town because their prices were slightly lower than those of the supermarkets in town and, most of all, because they issued you coupons that lowered the price of gasoline by 2 cents per gallon, from 25 to 23 cents.

One particular Wednesday morning Ralph and I got a pointed reminder of how our family could not afford to lose a single dime, quite literally. I was home that day and was going to drive my dad to work. As usual, he went out to the car to wait for me, but this time when I came out of the house I found him on all fours in the grass. He was brushing the grass gingerly with his hand and peering intently into the ground. It turned out he had dropped his dime, the only one he had, and the one he had planned to use to buy a soda to go with the bag lunch my mother had packed him. Right away, knowing that my father was also nervous about being late for work, I started to help him look for his dime, and soon Ralph came out and started to help too. We had gone from owning a small soda-bottling company to groveling for this dime for a single soda. Finally, we found the dime and all was well, but incidents like this stand out in your memory. Ralph and I call this the Lost Dime Story. It's part of family lore now.

So too is the car my parents bought once I went off to Florida

State with the gray '59 Chevy Bel Air. They knew a fellow Cuban exile working in Orlando as a busboy, and when he and his wife suddenly decided to try their luck in another city, he put his car up for sale. The car was an off-white '59 British Ford Consul that didn't even run. My dad bought it anyway, for seventy dollars, and took it to a tree-shade mechanic named Israel, also Cuban. The spring in the clutch was broken, meaning that the clutch pedal stayed down once your foot pressed it to the floor. To save my dad money, Israel jury-rigged the clutch, using nothing more than a rope. So you'd push the clutch pedal down, activating the clutch and temporarily disengaging the flywheel so you could shift gears, and then once you were in the new gear you would pull up on the rope Israel had attached to the pedal. Presto! The clutch and its now upright pedal were ready to be engaged again. Primitive doesn't even begin to describe this arrangement, but you know what? It worked. My father intensely disliked driving under normal circumstances, so you can imagine how he felt about this jalopy, having to pull up on that clutch rope like a fisherman yanking in his net. But he made it work, though Ralph, who had just gotten his license, drove the car much more frequently than Papi did (and much better, given the agility and adaptability of youth).

This car also burned oil like nobody's business. At that time you could buy used crankcase oil very cheaply in bulk containers at garages. My dad would keep this dirty used oil in containers in the trunk of his junker Ford Consul and top off the oil in the engine every morning. That resourcefulness makes me proud: my family made this wreck work for them. They were undaunted and adaptive to circumstances. They took the high road of self-sufficiency rather than the low road of self-pity.

That was typical of my father. He never gave up in America and always dug right in and worked things out, literally as well as figuratively. At T. G. Lee's Dairy he had to do all sorts of manual labor in addition to his veterinarian work. This meant he literally shoveled cow manure when he was idle. He did whatever was asked of him and never complained. He never held himself above such work just because he had a good professional education.

During this time, on my breaks home from school I would tell my dad all about my studies and my favorite professors and my job and my social life and my new friends. He would reciprocate with tales about his job. That's how I discovered he was hesitant and doubtful about taking the test for foreign veterinarians.

Instantly I recalled his wonderful talks with me in the months before I fled Cuba. For half a dozen years I had called on every ounce of guidance and advice he had given me then. And things were working out well for me. Now here was a real opportunity for role reversal. I definitely could empathize with my dad's hesitancy and his self-doubt. It was true that he faced a daunting language barrier even though he was an acclaimed and well-regarded veterinarian in his native language and his country of birth. But I knew in my heart that my dad could pass that foreign veterinarians' test. I also knew that this was exactly the kind of challenge he had prepared me to face in America. I knew what to do. I fed him back his own advice and his own life's philosophy just as he had imparted it to me, being careful not to cross the line into obviousness and thereby embarrass him.

At first he was dismissive of my encouragement to him. He thought he couldn't possibly pass the test. This particular mountaintop, he thought, was too high to summit. Not so, I told him. I urged him to work hard on his language skills and to start studying at night. On my subsequent trips home he confided to me that he was doing this. He studied for the test nights and weekends, just as he had studied diligently at the University of Havana back in the late 1930s. He no longer had his two great student buddies from those days to urge him on, but he studied hard, this time solo and isolated in more ways than one. Finally he told me he wanted to take the test. He would accept the challenge, and he would accept the results whatever they turned out to be; what happened would happen, he said, and that would be that.

And the first time out he passed the test.

My father had done far more for me than I could ever thank him or repay him for, but I welcomed this opportunity as a gift, as a small way to give back. To have a gift like that fall into your lap, to be able to give back to someone who gave you so much, especially one's parent, is a form of grace shining down on you, I'm convinced of it.

❖   ❖   ❖

THE TEST MY father passed, though it did not qualify him as a full veterinarian in the United States, did enable him to work with the Florida Department of Agriculture. With the blessing of Mr. Lee and Mr. Robinson at the dairy, he moved to a job in Gainesville as a sanitary inspector at a local poultry plant. There were ten inspectors working under him, and only he among them was certified by the state to make official calls. The plant kept him busy. It turned out seventy thousand chickens a day.

Of course the pay was much better than that at the dairy, but the new job presented the challenge of resettling the family. As a stopgap measure, my dad and I in the very early summer of 1968 moved in temporarily with Manolo Mesa, my dad's cousin, who had moved with his family to Gainesville. Manolo's son, Manolito, was the one who had come from his job as a bag boy at Winn-Dixie to meet my plane in Miami six years earlier. Sadly, Manolito had died in Vietnam a year earlier, fighting for his adoptive country even before becoming a citizen. My father and I moved in with the Mesas until we could find other living quarters so at least my dad could get started right away in his new Department of Agriculture job and I could find a summer job. I landed a job quickly, as my retail experience at Rutland's back in Orlando qualified me to sell men's furnishings in Wilson's department store in downtown Gainesville.

As soon as we settled in, my father and I started looking for housing in Gainesville. His salary had increased substantially and this new job was much more stable, so for the first time the idea of buying a house surfaced. Still, my father was doubtful we could pull it off. I encouraged him, though, and we both thought it would be great to own a house in the United States. Whatever thoughts of · going back to Cuba he may have harbored were fading by the day.

Our relatives the Mesas knew of a place just down the street that was up for sale. When my father and I went to look at it one day during our lunch hour, we knew that this house would be the one for our family. It had three bedrooms, one bath, a carport, and a fenced yard. It was, we realized, home.

Despite my father's initial doubts, we were able to buy the house. Between my father's savings and some of the money I had been able to set aside while working in Tallahassee, we managed to come up with a modest down payment.

My father was so proud. He would often say, "Can you believe we own a home? We have our own home in the United States." His pride permeated the whole family. I can't express what home ownership meant to us. It was the culminating achievement in giving us the sense of belonging and of putting down roots in our new culture. In the many years since, I have never forgotten what a milestone that was in all of our lives. Little did I know then that years later I would become the secretary of Housing and Urban Development (HUD), where I would be able to act on my passion for putting more Americans in homes they actually owned. It was, after all, an FHA (Federal Housing Administration) mortgage that allowed my family to own a home. Today, as a senator, I work constantly to improve and modernize the FHA because I know firsthand how effective it can be in making home ownership a reality for many Americans.

In mid-July 1968, two months after my father and I arrived in Gainesville, we were able to bring the whole family up there to move into our new house. We were thrilled—enough so that the inevitable hiccups on moving in just made us laugh.

Early on moving day my good friend Cesar Calvet and I rented a U-Haul truck to load up the family household in Orlando and drive it to Gainesville. Cesar's future wife, Olga, was lending a hand. We worked like dogs, and sweat was pouring off both Cesar and me on this scorching, terribly humid summer day. Finally we had loaded the truck with every piece of the household and were ready to go. But when I got in to drive, the brakes refused to work; they'd locked up completely. U-Haul sent out a mechanic, but he couldn't fix the brakes. We needed another truck. That meant Cesar and I had to unload the first truck and reload everything into the second. Remember, this was every stick of furniture, every lamp, every utensil, all the kitchenware, all the family's clothing—the whole works.

We finally managed to do it, but wouldn't you know it, we couldn't get the truck's back door closed. My little sister's bicycle, the very last thing to load, just wouldn't fit. Margarita panicked thinking her bike would have to be left behind. Cesar and I were both so exhausted by this time, having hauled mattresses and bedsteads and heavy dressers and a sofa and such, that we did whatever we could to fit it in. Ultimately we just kind of heaved it in there on top of the pile, shoved it forward, slammed the doors, and locked them. Sure enough, when we got to Gainesville and unloaded the truck, the bike was bent and inoperable. There was no way I was going to go off to college and leave my little sister with a broken bike and a broken heart. Not to mention me feeling permanently guilty. So I got the bike repaired right away and little Margarita was a happy camper in her new house with her hotshot bicycle.

The bike wasn't the only thing that got broken that summer.

While we were staying with the Mesas, I parked my '59 Chevy on the street in front of their house. One night a drunken driver plowed into it and kept right on going. When I came out in the morning the car was pretty well totaled. But we traced the drunk to a house right down the street, and after he owned up, the insurance company paid me what the car was worth. So I went with my father to University Chevrolet in Gainesville (with my dad, it was always Chevy). On the lot I spotted a beautiful 1964 Chevrolet Malibu two-door hardtop, gray on the top and burgundy on the bottom. I fell in love with it and bought that sporty little car on the spot. The car cost about $1,300, but I had the insurance money and I was also totally confident in my earning abilities now, since I had full command of the language. I knew I could work hard and pay that car loan off on time. So that summer my parents got their first mortgage and I got my first bank loan. We really were Americans now.

❖ ❖ ❖

AT THE END of the summer, happy and reassured that my family was all set to flourish in Gainesville, I went back to Tallahassee for my senior year. I had managed, besides chipping in for the down payment on my parents' house and buying the Malibu, to put aside most of the tuition money I would need my senior year from my job at Wilson's department store. And back on campus my job at the newspaper was waiting for me. That would go a long way with the car payments. I was also able to secure a student loan through the financial aid office at FSU.

Optimistic as ever, I still didn't have a glimmer of an idea that in my senior year the most life-enriching and momentous good fortune awaited me.

HOME: Buying our first house in America was a
huge milestone for the Martinez family.
Even the problems with the U-Haul truck
couldn't spoil our excitement.

Chapter 11

TURNING POINTS

I ARRIVED IN Tallahassee for my senior year feeling optimistic
about my family's future, even as my adoptive country was in a
time of turmoil. In that autumn of 1968 I was following the
presidential campaign as it heated up between Richard Nixon and
Hubert Humphrey. Like almost everyone else in the country I had
been glued to the TV watching the tumultuous events of the Democratic National Convention that summer in Chicago. I had seen
Mayor Richard Daley's police clash openly and violently with the
antiwar protestors in Grant Park, and when I arrived on campus the
air was still charged with a violent political divisiveness. There was
much talk about what the ultimate fate would be of the leaders of
the antiwar protest, dubbed the Chicago Seven. The war in Southeast Asia was tearing the country apart. For someone like me who
was now headlong involved in studying international affairs, political science, history, government, and economics, the whole country—
in fact the whole world—had turned into one bustling open-air
course with lots of lab work.

The debate about the war carried over onto Florida State's campus.

Small war protests and larger demonstrations were a regular occur-
rence, and occasionally there would be counterdemonstrations in favor
of the war, usually staged by Young Americans for Freedom (YAF).

I viewed all of this turmoil through the prism of my own experience with the cruelty and oppression of a Communist system. This
was only natural, since it was out of that hard experience in Cuba's
Communist regime that I had developed my passionate interest in
politics and history in the first place. So I was certainly not lining up
with the campus antiwar demonstrators. In fact, they reminded me
of my Cuban oppressors; long hair, beards, and olive drab fatigues
were not campus chic to me. Many students seemed to idealize the
Communists, including Che Guevara, who was then becoming a revolutionary icon in certain circles. Seeing Che's grungy face and
unkempt hair popping up on posters and T-shirts irritated me. As a
Cuban kid I had been victimized by Che's actions. I thought then (as
I think now) that the cult of Che was based on overwhelming
naïveté on the part of his idolaters.

With so much happening in the world, I wanted to understand
what had come before and what was driving all this upheaval. I
threw myself even deeper into studying history, government, and
economics. Luckily I had encountered a learned and wise professor named Richard B. Gray, whose area of expertise was Cuba. He
was my adviser, so we got to know each other well and would
often talk about his days in Cuba doing research before the Revolution. With Dr. Gray's guidance I grew to know my country's history far more thoroughly than I ever had before. But it wasn't just
Cuba's history he pointed me toward; as my faculty adviser he
directed much of my course selection so that I would have a solid
grounding in other subjects and be well rounded. Dr. Gray
inspired me to pursue new areas of interest and new academic

challenges. He was generous with his time and his advice, and I will be forever in his debt.

Another professor encouraged my growing interest in history and government as well. Like Dr. Gray, Ross Oglesby (for whom FSU's Student Union is named today) steered me to reading on my own, outside the assigned texts for a course. I began reading journals and reviews on foreign affairs and foreign governments. It was Dr. Oglesby who urged me to consider attending law school.

At home my father gave me a strong push in the same direction. He had overcome his moments of hesitancy about being able to pass the foreign veterinarians' test and so he had retaken with gusto his role as wise counselor to me. He was proud that I was doing well in school, that I had moved up to the head sales position at the school paper, and that I was earning more money. But he also told me that in this, my final year as an undergraduate, I had to think of what I would do to obtain a professional degree. He was unimpressed with a bachelor's degree as a full preparation for a career. Since he himself was a professional man, he wanted his sons to also be professional men. So he was delighted to hear that a professor had encouraged me to go to law school. Of course, everything in my educational portfolio—all of the courses on government, history, and economics—was pointing me toward law school also.

I realized that my dad and Dr. Oglesby were dead right, but this raised a whole new set of questions. Where would I get the money for law school? How many years of work would it take me to earn the tuition? What kind of work could I do to earn the tuition? As fate would have it, these questions led me to Tom Adams, Florida's secretary of state.

A former state senator, Adams as secretary of state was forging relationships between the state of Florida and the country of

Colombia, as part of the Alliance for Progress. The Alliance had begun in the Kennedy administration—just as Castro's Communist system was locking down on Cuba—to encourage North and South America to cooperate economically and enjoy mutual growth. Dr. Oglesby convinced me that I should contact Adams about a job. He knew that I had the language skills to help out with the Colombia initiative, and my studies had also prepared me to step into a role with Adams's office.

My professor set up an interview for me, and sure enough I got a job. I'd be working part-time during school as an administrative assistant for Adams, helping coordinate projects at Florida community colleges to enhance agricultural exchanges.

A job was not the only thing I got from Tom Adams. He and I also forged a friendship that would last until the day he died.

❖   ❖   ❖

IN MY LIFE I have never planned too far ahead. I was never one to sketch out every career choice in advance; I followed my passions, though never without prudent thought to what the next step would involve. I inherited this kind of relaxed assurance about the future from my parents, from my mom's faith and my dad's wise philosophy.

As my last semester of college began, in January 1969, I had only a touch of anxiety about what would come next. I had made the decision to go to law school, so now I could focus on this last bit of college life and all it had to offer. Tom Adams had also invited me to join his staff full-time after I graduated, so that resolved the question of what I would do to earn the money I needed to pay for law school. I would take a year off from school and work for him. I also knew that I would not be called to military service in Vietnam, even though I had registered for the draft even before I was officially sworn in as a citizen. Because of my lifelong high blood pressure, I had been classified as physically unfit for service.

By any measure, things were moving along wonderfully for me. I had good mentors and good friends. My friend Rick had graduated a year before me and had moved back to Orlando by this point, but I became very close with Ken Connor. A smart, slow-talking Southern guy from the north Florida town of Marianna, Ken had, like me, transferred from a junior college. By coincidence, or providence, he was in all my classes at FSU. He, too, was under Dr. Gray's guidance.

Ken and I were suffering from senioritis at this point, so we weren't too excited when Dr. Gray insisted that we take a course in anthropology before graduation. In fact, we protested and tried every persuasive argument that two budding barristers could present. Dr. Gray was unmoved. So, reluctantly, we signed up for Anthropology 316, "Pre-Columbian Anthropology." What I didn't know was that this class would have the greatest impact on my life of any other single event since I had arrived in the United States.

On the first day Ken and I sat at the back of the classroom, of course. Then, shortly after the class began, sheepishly into the front of the room stepped the person I would share my life with. She sat down in the one available seat in the front row. Ken and I immediately regretted our choice of going to the back of the room. I was struck by, and completely taken with, this beautiful young woman. The whole hour I stared at her from the back of the room. Ken was doing the same thing, I noticed. He and I exchanged glances.

"Do you know who she is?" I whispered.

"No."

We stared at each other. We both knew this was someone we wanted to meet, but how?

When class ended, a couple of students lingered to ask questions. Ken and I had no questions to ask but we lingered too because the late arrival to class had a lot of questions she wanted answered: What books were required reading? What additional reading was recommended? When were midterms? We stayed long enough to catch her name, Kitty Tindal, but were not clever enough to start a conversation. I was head over heels and Ken knew it. By the next time the class met, we engineered our seating and managed to sit on either side of this completely uninterested, cute, and clever new classmate.

We were up to the challenge. In a fast break, two on offense can always beat one defender. The ice wall seemingly surrounding this beautiful young woman would be chiseled down thanks to the numbers advantage, Ken and I versus Kitty. She had to talk to us if we kept talking to her, we figured. And she did. But although polite and friendly, she was nevertheless reserved.

The classroom chats continued for days until Ken, knowing that this beautiful coed was all I talked about, pressured me to act. In his north Florida drawl, Ken finally said, "Mel, either you ask her out or I will."

I was paralyzed, infatuated, and shy. But yes, the time had come.

I asked Kitty to go for a Coke at the Student Union after class. Gulp!

"Thanks, but I don't drink them," came the still icy reply.

Digging deep, I managed to say, "How about a Sprite?"

This got only a slightly less icy, "No, thanks. I just had a Sprite right before class."

We were getting somewhere, I thought. This wasn't a flat no! She was maybe probing, testing? Maybe softening? I smiled.

With my brain spinning, I said, "Well, how about an ice cream cone?"

"Sure, I love ice cream," came the reply, and now there was a smile on her face, too.

Wow! I took a deep breath and told myself to stay cool. And the rest, well, the rest is a very happy history.

KITTY: I'll always thank Professor Gray for
insisting I take that anthropology class.

Chapter 12

KITTY

T O T H I S D A Y I consider my first date with Kitty to have been that day in January 1969 when we strolled to the Florida State Student Union after class for ice cream. Whenever I tell people that, Kitty corrects me, saying it was simply a "visit" over ice cream, far too informal to be a date.

But to me, that first encounter was magical. I was taken with Kitty from the beginning. Our conversation flowed easily and we laughed a lot. We had come from very different worlds and that gave us a lot to talk about. Even before we shared that ice cream, I had felt exhilarated when I noticed her in church. Standing in the back of the church, I looked forward toward the altar and suddenly saw her sitting in one of the front pews. Immediately I was elated to realize that she too was Catholic. Yet, reserved as ever, I didn't approach her after mass, feeling that to do so might simply be too forward.

So I was thrilled when our first post-class stroll together led to more. Spring was then in bloom, and for the next few weeks we would meet up after anthropology and enjoy the pleasant afternoons together. As we walked we'd discuss what we were learning in class. We even made a few afternoon visits to a nearby artist our professor had recommended, an older gentleman who made exact replicas of pre-Columbian pottery. This artist had actually lived in Cuba for a while, so he and I spoke about the country's history and our experiences there. Naturally, these discussions led Kitty and me to talk about Cuba and my life there. She was even interested in my native language. She had been taking Spanish courses at FSU for about a year and a half and had taken summer courses before that, so on our afternoon walks she began practicing her Spanish with me.

Encouraged by our afternoons together, about a month later I asked for and was granted what she considers a formal date— grabbing pizza, in the evening, of course.

Only later did Kitty fill me in on why she had been reserved with me in those early days: she had another romantic interest at the time. I was so taken with her that I had never noticed that she wore a pin—her boyfriend's fraternity pin. She confided to me later that she had told him all about me and about our visits with the artist. He didn't like it, but she assured him that I was only a friend, because, at that point, that's all I was. But by the time I asked her out for the more formal date, she had returned his pin and broken up with him.

That first "real date" ignited a whirlwind courtship. We quickly became nearly inseparable whenever we were free of school commitments or work obligations. We spent as much time together as possible, going for rides in rural areas around Tallahassee and to movies, concerts, plays, and, of course, Seminoles football games. Many of these dates ended at night with a milk shake at the Sweet Shop on the FSU campus. The more we got to know each other, the more we fell in love.

❖　❖　❖

I GRADUATED FROM Florida State in June of '69, and soon thereafter I made the formal trip home with Kitty to be introduced to her family in Mobile, Alabama. Before that first meeting I suffered some uneasiness. Coming from a different ethnic group, I had anxieties above and beyond the usual doubts every suitor has. At least I had Sidney Poitier to lean on: just a couple of years earlier he had walked through the fire for all suitors from a different ethnic group in the hit movie *Guess Who's Coming to Dinner.*

Also, it helped that Kitty's mother, Polly, and I are both talkers. Almost as soon as we met we fell into a long and mutually enchanting conversation that is still going on. Another reason Polly and I bonded is that we're both early risers. Kitty in those days loved to sleep late, as did her sister, Deanna, and her brother, Chris. So Kitty's dad, Larry, would be off at work and the others would still be asleep, and Polly and I would have the kitchen to ourselves to chat over breakfast and coffee. There was no friction at all. In fact, Kitty later told me that Polly had joked that if Kitty didn't marry me, she would. I was blessed to have had a very good relationship with Polly from the beginning.

Kitty's dad was a little different. Larry was harder to get to know, a strong and silent type. Polly told me years later that during my first visit Larry took a hard look at me, wondering as fathers have since the dawn of time if this suitor was worthy of his daughter's attention, let alone her hand in marriage. Looking for drawbacks in me, he was only able to mutter to Polly, "He's just too nice."

But if I didn't immediately have the warm connection with Larry that I shared with Polly, I had enormous respect for his character and accomplishments. Larry Tindal was Exhibit A of a self-reliant American, and he had decency to burn and a sense of fair play that never wavered. A survivor of the Depression and World War II, he was a self-made man: he had won a full scholarship to Auburn University in engineering and, while there, joined ROTC. Upon graduating in 1942 he entered the army as a second lieutenant and rose to the rank of major within the next three years, a meteoric ascension for a guy who had not come out of West Point. After the war he went to work as an engineer at Westinghouse in Pittsburgh, and that's where he met Polly in 1946. They were married the following year.

Slowly Larry and I grew to appreciate what we had in common. He was, first of all, a devout Catholic, having converted after being raised as a Baptist. Also, like a lot of Southern boys, he loved to hunt, and so did I. We went out bird hunting together a few times, just as I'd gone bird hunting back in Cuba with my dad, and I loved every minute of it. Larry really knew what he was doing out there with a shotgun and a trained bird dog.

Larry and I both loved to talk cars, too. In those days I was proud of my Chevy Malibu. Larry knew it, and he showed a lot about his character when Kitty and I had a problem with the car. Kitty was doing community work in the La Petite Marching Corps and participated in a fund-raiser in which they were selling doughnuts by the dozen. Using my Malibu for distribution, she loaded the backseat with about twenty boxes holding a dozen Krispy Kreme doughnuts each. Only my car was not air-conditioned and it was steaming hot that day. The heat trapped in the car melted the sugar on the doughnuts and it seeped through the thin boxes. The upholstery in the backseat was ruined, all glazed over with melted sugar. I was already, after only a few months, deeply in love with Kitty. Still, this strained matters a mite. That's when Kitty borrowed the car and drove home for the weekend to Mobile. Larry Tindal took one look and viewed what had happened with horror. He drove the car straight to a body shop and had the seats redone. They were as good as new. He was that kind of guy.

❖   ❖   ❖

I TOOK KITTY home to Gainesville to meet my family that autumn. Before they actually met her, my parents had been slightly apprehensive, wondering why I would not want to marry a nice Cuban girl. My parents weren't upset, exactly, just a little mystified. But even before they met her they knew that I was very much in love with Kitty.

Ralph, the family historian, tells me with a chuckle about the Sunday night during that autumn of '69 that I didn't call home. Like the Martinez Sunday Night Dinner, my Sunday night call was sacred ritual. But I was with Kitty on this particular Sunday evening and somehow in all the romantic rush completely forgot to call home. As Ralph tells me, my parents turned to each other when it had clearly grown too late for me to call, realizing as they did that I had actually missed my unmissable call. My father said, "This girlfriend Mel has is serious. This must be the one." My mother, sensitive and intuitive as ever, replied, "I bet he will be bringing her home soon."

She was right. And any skepticism my family may have felt about Kitty disappeared over the first weekend they spent with her. Within fifteen minutes she had charmed them all, including my brother and sister. Margarita, who was approaching her ninth birthday, felt that she had acquired the big sister she'd always wanted. My parents especially loved that Kitty could converse with them in Spanish.

For her part, Kitty appreciated my mother's sensitivity. Even though Kitty was able to converse in Spanish, there was always a cacophony of Spanish conversation in our house—actually, several simultaneous conversations most of the time, overlapping and alternating and preempting one another. My mother noticed that Kitty's eyes began to glaze over after an hour or so of trying to translate all of it. She took Kitty by the arm and asked if she wouldn't like to lie down and have a nap, which was exactly what Kitty needed. Kitty claims that my mother is extra sensitive to other people's wants and needs and moods, and she may be right. In any case, for all the years they've known each other, my wife and my mother have gotten along splendidly.

❖   ❖   ❖

BY THAT AUTUMN Kitty and I were deeply committed to each other. Having graduated, I was working full-time on the staff of the Florida secretary of state, Tom Adams, in order to save up for law school. This type of diplomatic and governmental work was exciting for me. I would travel with Secretary Adams when he went to Colombia. Doing this work, I finally received a real payoff for all the struggles and embarrassments I had endured trying to learn English in those frustrating first months at Bishop Moore. I ended up doing simultaneous translation for Adams, just as I had for my father when he started working at the dairy in Orlando. When I started translating, all my earlier experiences struggling to put English words to their Spanish equivalents, and vice versa, would flood back on me and stand me in good stead.

Kitty, meanwhile, was in her junior year at Florida State. So while I was preparing for law school, she was working toward her undergraduate degree. And now we were focused on our future *together*. Finally, that Christmas of '69 I had a formal chat with her father, picked out a ring, and asked her to marry me. We didn't want a long engagement, and we didn't want to stage an overly elaborate wedding ceremony. Kitty and Polly went to work making plans, and arrangements were soon set for us to be married that coming June in Mobile.

An odd thing happened while Kitty and I were visiting in Mobile with her family over that Christmas when we became engaged. We laugh about it now, but at the time it was disconcerting. I was out dove hunting with Larry, having a great day while totally oblivious of the drama playing out back at the Tindal house. Right at that time

Castro had stage-managed a series of plane hijackings in which the hijackers would demand to be flown to Cuba, ostensibly seeking political asylum in enlightened Cuba from the evil *yanquis*. A fellow known only as "M. Martinez," and roughly fitting my physical description, had hijacked a plane that day and demanded it be flown to Havana. Naturally, the FBI had gleaned the files for all "M. Martinez" candidates, and because I matched up physically with this culprit, they wanted to check me out. When the FBI agents tracked me to my apartment in Tallahassee, my roommate at the time, a good friend named Johnny Harris, ever helpful, "gave me up." He told the FBI I was visiting my girlfriend's family in Mobile.

So while Larry and I were out walking in a dove field on a beautiful winter afternoon, Kitty's sister, Deanna, a seventeen-year-old high school senior at the time—and, like most high school seniors, a bit ditzy in a charming way—answered the door when the FBI agent knocked. Holding the door open, Deanna listened attentively as the agent explained why he needed to talk to me, "M. Martinez." When they finished, Deanna looked him straight in the eye and said, "Oh, gosh, I don't think he'd ever do anything like that." While she was surely persuasive, the agent was not satisfied, and when I returned to the house I had to have an interview with him in the living room of my in-laws-to-be. Kitty's family was in my corner right from the start, but this incident was a reminder that they were welcoming someone from a different ethnic background.

❖ ❖ ❖

WHEN OUR WEDDING weekend rolled around in June 1970, our two extended families converged for the first time. Many of my relatives made the trip to Mobile, and they and Kitty's family all seemed to blend in happily and well. Of course there was a little bit of a language barrier but nothing major, since by then nearly all my family members had been in America long enough to manage in English. And Kitty could converse with them in Spanish, a quality all my relatives found endearing, just as my parents had.

With her usual determination Kitty had prevailed in altering the plans for just how and where our wedding would take place. Back in the early 1950s Polly had been instrumental in helping a young priest named Father Sullivan found their parish church, Holy Family. Father Sullivan had since become Monsignor Sullivan. Both he and Polly had assumed that Kitty would want to be married at Holy Family. Of course Kitty badly wanted Monsignor Sullivan to perform the ceremony and preside over our nuptial mass as celebrant, but she insisted that all of this take place at the gorgeous old white St. Joseph's Chapel at Spring Hill College, a Jesuit institution and the oldest college in the state. Kitty is very proud of the Catholic heritage of Mobile, which dates back to the establishment of the city in 1710 by Sieur de Bienville, whose retinue included pioneering Jesuits. For the next nine years, from 1710 to 1719, Mobile was the capital of French Louisiana, and this is the reason the Mardi Gras in Mobile is the oldest in America. At any rate, Kitty had her heart set on being married in St. Joseph's Chapel, which sits on the Spring Hill campus at the terminus of an avenue of live oaks. Finally she was able to persuade the good monsignor that although it is customary for a bride to be married in her home parish, it wouldn't hurt if she shifted our nuptials ever so slightly to the chapel at Spring Hill.

The rehearsal dinner was my family's event and, although it was a struggle financially, it was very nicely done at the Bienville Club. The wedding went off beautifully with Ralph as my best man and Kitty's best friend, Gail Walton, as her matron of honor, and her sister, Deanna, as the maid of honor; Margarita served as a junior bridesmaid, while Chris, who was close to my sister's age, was an altar boy. It was a real family affair.

It was hot in the lovely but not air-conditioned chapel. After the reception at the Women's Club of Mobile, Kitty and I climbed into our car, a little beige Volkswagen that had the usual spray-painted windows and ribbons and cans attached to the rear bumper. Margarita and Chris, who had become fast friends, had organized that part of the celebration. Kitty and I pulled away from Mobile and set out on our rambling honeymoon excursion. We were blissfully, ecstatically happy.

We traveled to the mountains of North Carolina and then, four days later, pulled into Atlanta for the night. We intended to have dinner with my aunt Yolanda and my mother, who was there visiting her sister. We had just driven down from Gatlinburg, Tennessee, and its astonishingly beautiful views of the Great Smokies. When I called my aunt to let her know we were in town and all set to meet her and my mother for our prearranged dinner that night, I was shocked to hear that Polly had been desperately trying to reach us for the past two days. Kitty called her mother and was devastated to learn that we had to get to Mobile right away.

Tragedy had struck. Kitty's dad had suffered a massive aneurysm.

A NEW DIRECTION: Working for Florida's
secretary of state, Tom Adams (shown
here with me in Colombia), inspired
my interest in public service.

Chapter 13

NEW HOMES

K ITTY AND I were stunned when we received news of Larry's illness. The company he had worked for loyally for so many years, International Paper, offered to fly us down to Mobile on the company plane, but we elected to drive instead. Shattered by the news, we intended to use the driving time to think and catch our breath. Besides, we wanted to get moving as quickly as possible. So within about five hours we were at the hospital in Mobile.

We were grateful to be able to render whatever love and support we could to Polly and to Kitty's younger sister and brother. Kitty and I walked the hospital grounds with Polly between us as we discussed the various medical options, all of which were grim. One doctor felt there was nothing to be done. Another doctor, a younger and more positive one, proposed doing a cranial operation or pursuing a new drug regimen. In the end the younger doctor operated, but it was to no avail. About ten days after the operation, Larry suffered a massive stroke. He died on June 30, just seventeen days after we were married.

Having regrets in life can be a trap, and I have few, but I do regret that I never had the chance to get to know my father-in-law better. He was a terrific human being. In the last conversation I had with Larry he was quite concerned to know whether I had remembered to have the oil changed in our Volkswagen. It was overdue. He was always thinking of others, right to the last. Before we left, when the two of us were alone, I said to Larry, "I will always take care of Kitty."

When your father's funeral follows your own wedding within three weeks it is tough to handle, but with her usual stoicism and aplomb Kitty came through it intact, striving always to put comforting her mother and her siblings before her own crushing sense of grief. Her dignity during this ordeal touched me deeply, and sharing so much pain early in our marriage brought us closer together and gave us added strength. For a short while after the funeral I found my role as husband augmented by that of temporary father while Kitty struggled to adjust to the horrible, wrenching, and sudden loss of the strong shoulders and guidance of her father. I was only too glad to be there for her until she fully rebounded from this catastrophic loss. She said that God had been good to her in not taking her father from her until she was safely in my arms.

❖　　❖　　❖

ABOUT A WEEK after Larry's funeral, when Kitty was satisfied that the Tindal household was stabilized enough for us to leave, we drove back down to Tallahassee and plunged into our new life as a married couple. Tom Adams had tempted me with an offer to stay on with his staff, but as much as I loved the job, I held fast to my plan. I was set to begin law school at Florida State that fall, while Kitty was entering her final year as an undergraduate.

As soon as we got back to Tallahassee, Kitty set about fixing up our living quarters in married student housing at FSU. She was keeping busy, a time-honored way to blunt grief's edge. The married-student housing, in Alumni Village, was fairly spartan, but Kitty used her imagination and what few dollars we could spare to make it comfortable. Our next-door neighbors were another newlywed couple: Ed Anton was also an incoming law student, but the great surprise was that his new bride, Dora, was a childhood friend of mine from Sagua la Grande. During our time in law school Ed and Dora became good friends with whom we socialized a lot.

Kitty and I had exactly $1,200 when we married, the money I had saved by working for Tom Adams, and I had spent $200 on our honeymoon. That left us an even thousand, not enough to make it through a year no matter how conservative with money we were. I was determined to make ends meet because—Polly laughs about it to this day—I had used every ounce of salesmanship in me to convince Larry and her to allow Kitty to marry me. I was not about to fail them or their daughter. Kitty understood that the first year of law school is critical, and she could not have been more supportive through that extraordinarily challenging year. She spent a good deal of time studying too, and she accepted the fact that our social life was limited by my massive workload and our scarce funds. We did continue to go to the big FSU football games, and later I introduced her to going to basketball and baseball games. But we seldom went to a movie, let alone a play or a concert. The budget simply wouldn't stretch that far.

We got through that year using maximum care and discretion with our meager supply of money and with help from student loans. As a first-year law student, I was discouraged by the law school from having a job, but Kitty worked afternoons and weekends as a book-keeper for a department store. She would walk quickly by the racks of clothes on the way to her office, not wanting to be tempted to buy something we could not afford. Whenever my dad came to visit he brought us bags and bags of frozen chicken, which he bought at the plant with his employee's discount. Kitty and I ate chicken that year to the point where we nearly started to cluck and sprout feathers. But for us, it was like manna from Heaven. That was an arduous year, with both of us shouldering heavy workloads and with Kitty having to endure the lingering grief of her father's loss, but we pulled through it.

Although law school was difficult, I took to it quickly. I was lucky to have my good friend Ken Connor showing me the ropes. He had started law school right after we graduated from college together, so he was a year ahead of me. With Ken helping me out, I grew increasingly excited about becoming a lawyer. The more legal education I acquired, the more appealing the profession became.

I got more practical exposure to the law when Ken encouraged me to try out for the school's Moot Court team, of which he was a member. This was a prestigious group on campus that competed in mock appellate arguments against the best legal debaters from other Florida law schools. I knew that the selection process for the team was intensely competitive, but along with my law school study partner Jim Corrigan, another neighbor in Alumni Village, I decided to go for it. It was a survival-of-the-fittest process, so Jim and I were thrilled when we both made the team. We were two of only three first-year students to be chosen.

My excitement was genuine, but when I thought about the challenges I would face in these simulated courtroom settings, my confidence level was not high. Although I had been translating for high-level government officials, I had been speaking English for only nine years and wasn't sure I would be able to speak effectively off-the-cuff under such pressure. But Kitty's faith in me was unbreakable, and Ken's support never wavered either. Ken oriented me on what to expect and what to do. So, with the same competitive spark that had spurred me on in sports, I went at it all-out.

Moot Court, I found, gives you the kind of practical experience for courtroom advocacy and argument that aspiring doctors get from serving a demanding internship. I threw myself into the experience, trying to learn every nuance and technique I could. I began heading to the State Court and to the State Supreme Court to watch trials and track arguments. I would sit with the audience and simply observe and absorb. The competitions were what I loved the most. Trying cases and making arguments and competing on behalf of clients was right up my alley. I knew by then that I wanted to be an advocate, a trial lawyer, and each and every Moot Court competition only reinforced this conviction.

The big payoff came at the end of the year, when I attended the Florida Bar Association Convention at Miami's Doral Hotel to compete in the state Moot Court competition against the other Florida law schools. Ken, Jim, and I went to Miami with our faculty adviser, Bill VanDercreek, and the other team members. Jim and I were partners, and we won the competition for best brief and lost in the finals for the best argument. As first-year students we were elated to have done so well, and also to have been able to showcase our talents. Prominent lawyers and jurists from around the state served as judges for the competition, and we understood that performing well in front of them could open doors for us after law school.

Now more than ever, I knew that the law was the right place for me.

❖   ❖   ❖

AT CHRISTMAS 1970, the first holidays after Kitty and I married, we naturally went to Mobile to be with the Tindals, to help everyone over the grief of losing Larry six months earlier. The way the Tindal family conducted themselves and bounced back was amazing. Without a doubt, all of us still felt Larry's loss every day. Earlier that autumn, a crushed Polly had even asked her daughter Deanna not to go off to Auburn as she had been slated to do, but instead to live at home and take her first year of college at Mobile's own University of South Alabama. This Deanna readily did, and together she and her mom saw Chris through his last year of elementary school. By Christmas, the strength of the Tindal family was shining through, as Kitty and I witnessed.

Polly had steeled herself and taken a full-time teaching job offered by her parish school, where she had served as a substitute teacher from time to time; she would teach there for years to come. The family had been rocked by Larry's death, but life slowly became more stable.

❖   ❖   ❖

AFTER ONE YEAR in student housing, Kitty and I moved to an apartment building, the Stadium Apartments. The only reason we could swing this change was that I became the building manager, and part of my compensation was a free apartment—something we really needed, since we were out of money. Kitty and I divided the responsibilities. She dealt with the tenants and was in charge of showing the units, renting them out, and then collecting the rents. I did the maintenance, gathering the trash and putting it out for removal, cleaning the pool, and collecting the money from the in-house Laundromat. I was also the handyman. I would do all the minor plumbing, like changing washers and freeing clogged drains and toilets; I also took care of all the light fixtures, both inside and out.

The job was a great relief financially, because in addition to getting the rent-free apartment, I also received $100 a month, just what my job on the school newspaper had paid me. By this point, too, Kitty had graduated from Florida State and begun working in the state's Department of Commerce. Tom Adams, who had become lieutenant governor by then, was kind enough to make the introductions and set up the interviews for her. So compared to our first year of marriage, we were in a much less tenuous financial position. With Kitty's job, my income, the free housing, and my student loans, we were able to finance law school. And I never minded the menial tasks I had to do as building manager. They relaxed me, actually. As I replaced a faucet or repaired a wall sconce, I would review cases in my head or rehearse arguments for Moot Court. When I wasn't performing maintenance duties, I could study in the tiny manager's office in the back of the laundry. It was a great place to get work done because the drone of the washers blocked out noises.

Stadium Apartments was nothing fancy but we had a great time living there. In our little apartment we hosted some memorable dinners—yes, they always featured chicken—and threw a few modest parties for our friends, including, Ken, Jim, Ed and Dora, and lots of other law school classmates. The apartment building sat on a hill overlooking the FSU football stadium—hence the name Stadium Apartments (now it's a Florida State athletic dorm called Burt Reynolds Hall). So on a beautiful spring day we could walk down the hill and watch spring football practice, or could walk a few more paces and take in an FSU baseball game.

The university atmosphere, when participated in properly, is hard to beat. It offers great fun and great friendships. It was heavenly for Kitty and me.

❖　　❖　　❖

THERE WAS ANOTHER significant development during my second year of law school. One day, thinking about the future, I realized it was time to become a citizen of the United States of America. Though I felt deeply about my adoptive country, I had not taken the final formal steps toward citizenship. Now I went forward with the process and the paperwork, which finally culminated with the swearing-in ceremony held one afternoon at the Federal Courthouse in Tallahassee. It was not a big ceremony like the ones I have since attended as a guest speaker while a Cabinet officer and a senator, but it was full of great meaning. Kitty was the only one in the audience for me, but it meant everything to have her there.

That night, to celebrate, Kitty prepared an all-American meal of hot dogs and homemade apple pie. I couldn't help but reflect on what had brought me to this transformation. My life's journey was a classic immigrant story. I had gone from being an accidental visitor to being a resident and, finally, a citizen. The oath of American citizenship requires a renunciation of all past loyalties and an acceptance of the new one. It had taken ten years but now I was an American, and not by an accident of birth but by choice. The sense of happiness, of patriotism, and of finally belonging that citizenship conferred on me was wonderful. The blessings of America are many, and the opportunities available in this unique American experiment in freedom and democracy are unparalleled. Ever since that day I have felt extremely fortunate that I am an American citizen. The desire to give something back to a great nation lies at the heart of what would lead me to my late-in-life vocation for public service.

❖　❖　❖

I SOMETIMES THINK of mentors as a blessed daisy chain, a kind of secular rosary. Because my own father was absent for my first four years in America and then handicapped by the language difficulty, I often think how lucky I've been when it comes to having mentors.

At Bishop Moore I had Coach Larry Mullan. At Orlando Junior College I had Dr. Rickert and Professor Zimorski. As an undergrad at FSU I had Drs. Gray and Oglesby. It was Dr. Oglesby who led me to Secretary of State Tom Adams, who exposed me to the kinds of international engagement and cooperation that I wanted to participate in later in my career.

And as a mentor Tom Adams was legendary. I was one among a legion of former Adams staffers who went on to achieve significant accomplishments in state government. It's no accident he had so many protégés. He was an inspirational man, a kind man, a man who took a personal interest in others without expectation of gain for himself. He did altruistic things reflexively.

He even gave me marital advice, saying that Kitty and I were obviously deeply in love and urging us to protect our mutual passion, to nurture it and make it grow throughout our lives. Though his later career was somewhat blemished when he was faulted for poor judgment, I still admired him greatly. He had a preternatural ability to connect with a crowd. In my political life I have always tried to emulate that. He could motivate and excite people. He had a highly developed sense of mission, which I think is an essential quality for any truly gifted public official to have. I feel privileged to have known him. I also felt proud when, in early 2006, the dying Tom Adams wrote me a letter asking me to eulogize him at his funeral. He passed away shortly thereafter, and I was honored to deliver the formal eulogy.

Yet another mentor was Bill VanDercreek, the faculty adviser to our Moot Court team. Professor VanDercreek was not only a member of the law school faculty but also an accomplished trial lawyer. I was able to work for him as his research assistant, which brought in much-needed income to supplement my stipend from managing the

Stadium Apartments. It also enhanced my legal skills and drove home the lesson that the substance and fine points of advocacy cannot all be learned in law school.

From one mentor to the next, I have continually seen good fortune shine on me.

❖   ❖   ❖

EVEN MORE GRATIFYING to me than my own good fortune was that of my family.

By 1971 nearly everyone on my dad's side of the family had fled Cuba and had been living in Florida for at least three or four years, some longer.

Plus, my immediate family was booming along. My father had the solid job with the Florida Department of Agriculture. My mom was enjoying herself running the household and occasionally earning extra money by working out of our house as a hairdresser. Ralph was an undergraduate living at the ATO fraternity house at the University of Florida right there in Gainesville; he would frequently bring half the fraternity home for a great Cuban meal prepared by our mother. And Margarita, now a sixth grader, had blossomed into a happy, vivacious girl who was active in school and would bounce into a room with a smile. With both Ralph and me out of the house, she was more than ever the spark of unblemished joy for my parents. She was a joy to me, too. It was just a great pleasure to watch Margarita grow before my eyes and to be the big brother to her that I hadn't been able to be during all those years of separation.

Kitty and I spent Christmas of 1971 with my folks. One especially poignant moment during that holiday season stands out for me. It made me realize that my family too felt the sense of belonging that had been solidified for me when I met Kitty.

Christmas Eve, called Noche Buena in Spanish, is a big night for Cubans. When we all lived back in Cuba it was traditional for my grandmother Graciela to host a feast on that night. For days before the event my dad would carefully observe the pigs he went to inspect and then would select the biggest and best one to roast on Noche Buena. Then, when the big event arrived, the pig would roast all day long, and the whole extended family would get dressed in their best and gather at my grandmother's large apartment in down-town Sagua la Grande. The lavish feast would feature the roasted pig and other traditional sumptuous food as well—black beans and rice, yucca with mojo sauce, and a selection of different *turrones,* or nougats, from Spain. Just as my memories of Cuban summers center on the beach, Noche Buena is what I think of when I remember Christmastime in Cuba.

That's why Christmas Eve of 1971 was so wonderful for me. All of the extended family gathered to celebrate Noche Buena traditionally again, only this time we crammed into grandmother Graciela's small apartment in Little Havana in Miami. But we were all there, the whole extended family, all the uncles, aunts, cousins, in-laws, everyone. At one point I glanced across the room and saw Kitty conversing with my grandmother and my mother. Kitty was now part of the mix and she fit right in due to her great effort at speaking Spanish. In the Cuban tradition of the firstborn I had always been Graciela's favorite grandchild. She and I shared a special relationship.

What mattered most was that our whole family was together again at this special time of year, just like old times. But now we were *Americans.* Our Christmas tradition was still there, only in a new place. Traditions can be assailed but not eradicated; we simply transplanted them. We did not have the material things we had in Cuba, but we had one another, we had our traditions, and we had our freedom. It was clear to me that my family had embraced our new beginning and appreciated our sense of belonging.

❖   ❖   ❖

KITTY AND I enjoyed a full life while I was in law school, with great friends and exciting new opportunities and learning experiences. Yet, like all good things, it was coming to an end. It was time for us to look forward, not back. And around the corner lurked real life.

In my last year at FSU I began to worry about interviewing for a job and planning for our future. Uncertainty lay ahead—there was that word again. The feelings conjured by this uncertainty were reminiscent of those I experienced when leaving Camp St. John for the foster home.

During my final year of law school the Moot Court competition took place in Orlando, at Walt Disney World. Sitting in the audience that day was June Berkmeyer, my second foster mother. She was so proud to watch me argue my case, and of course she thought I should have won hands down. (I didn't, but Jim Corrigan and I did perform well in the competition.) Seeing June again reminded me of what a strong connection I had to Orlando, even though I had now spent several years in Tallahassee and the rest of my family had moved on to Gainesville. That connection would prove important when it came time for the next step after law school.

Ken Connor, who had graduated a year before me, suggested I interview with the Orlando firm of Billings, Frederick, Wooten & Honeywell. Ken had opted not to go with Billings because he was (and still is) a small-town guy who wanted to avoid Orlando, but he convinced me to look hard at the firm. Sure enough, I really connected with Billings when I interviewed. When they offered me a job, I accepted. Although I did have another job offer for slightly more money, I simply felt more comfortable going with this fine firm of great people and talented lawyers.

Plus there was a bonus with this decision: I was going home to Orlando.

MARGARITA: My little sister and I shortly after she
arrived in America. Making up for lost time,
I doted on Margarita.

Chapter 14

MARGARITA

THINGS HAD BROKEN just right for me again. Fresh out of law school I was able to join a very well respected firm, and better yet, I would be working in my hometown. Being back in Orlando charged my batteries, and introducing Kitty to the town was fun. Before we knew it, we were moving into our first house together, an affordable place in Winter Park, just north of Orlando. My former foster father Jim Berkmeyer, who was a successful real estate broker, found us this nice home, and Kitty's grandfather floated us a bridge loan to help with the down payment. It was another milestone for us in building our lives together—our first home, our first mortgage.

Billings, Frederick, Wooten & Honeywell was a medium-sized firm with a strong history in the Orlando community, and it proved to be the perfect fit for me. I took to practicing law as I had taken to baseball as a boy. I loved it. I couldn't get enough of being immersed in it. The travails you hear sometimes from young lawyers didn't apply to me. Of course the hours were long, but I was used to working hard from having put myself through school. And yes, the research could seem endless, but it was tedious only if you lost sight of the objective. I was helping to win the cases for our clients, and since the firm represented individuals and not big corporations, I valued the opportunity right from the start to have early client contact and to learn from it.

I was passionate about my work. I did legwork too, going out to interview witnesses and experts, acquiring a feel for the "real" side of being a lawyer. Before I knew it I was assisting in taking depositions and learning the ins and outs of trial preparation from the partners in the firm, all of them seasoned trial lawyers. All that courtroom preparation was especially worth it to me, because I got to attend the trials and assist the partners. My first experience "second-chairing" a trial and actually going inside the bar in the courtroom was thrilling.

I had found my métier. I was born to be a lawyer. Like my father, I had the happiest of all things happen to me: I loved my chosen profession. No one believes this of lawyers, because our services are priced high, but some of us actually practice law for the love of it. I especially valued the way being a lawyer enabled me to help others. My grandfather Melquiades had seen helping others as a responsibility. He not only employed quite a few men with his soda-bottling factory, he also was a Rotarian in Sagua la Grande, served simultaneously as a municipal delegate and as an administrator of the municipal government, and even stepped in as interim mayor once when the sitting mayor became incapacitated. What's more, he established a children's pavilion in Playa Uvero, the town where he had built the family beach house.

My dad had picked up this tradition as well, always helping out in one way or another in Sagua. When he walked into town to socialize with his friends at the café, he would always listen to their problems and help out whenever and however he could. He continued this tradition in America. Even after my parents moved to

Gainesville, my dad never lost contact with Orlando's growing Cuban-American community or with the congregants of St. James Cathedral. He was always trying to help people out with their problems.

Seeing what my father prioritized had a profound impact on me. He also made sure I continued the tradition of helping others. Whenever he visited Orlando, he would volunteer me to all of his friends. "I'll ask my son the lawyer and get back to you." "Take that to my older son, Mel, and see what he thinks. He's a lawyer and knows about such things." I ended up reading leases and insurance policies, advising on house closings and wills, and doing other such legal work for my father's friends. It was always pro bono, since the people my dad referred to me didn't have the money to pay a lawyer. It was just like those little scratch farmers back in Sagua with one cow who would pay my father for veterinary work months later with two chickens or some fruits and vegetables left by the back door.

Another reason I knew that Billings, Frederick, Wooten & Honeywell was the right place for me was that the firm did not emphasize work above everything else. Early in my time at the firm, Jerry Billings, a name partner who was no longer that active in the practice, gave me some valuable advice about balance in life: first, faith; second, family; and third, work.

Kitty and I were gratified to see things going well in our personal lives and with our families. Kitty kept busy between working a regular job at an insurance company and attending school, doing work toward a master's degree in English Education. She was meeting my old buddies from high school like Gary Preisser, Rick Steinke, and Cesar Calvet—and their wives, because by this time they too were married. We began hosting small dinner parties at home for these and other friends—and it wasn't chicken only anymore, now that I was earning a nice income at the law firm. We also had the time and money to socialize more on the weekends, going out to dinners, shows, and movies with other couples. Quite often we would travel back to Tallahassee for football games and impromptu weekend reunions with old law school buddies. No longer were we limited to cheap wine and cheese parties before and after big football games. Kitty even had a wardrobe that no longer required her to alternate two pairs of slacks.

Back home in Mobile, Kitty's mother, Polly, had matters well in hand. Kitty's sister, Deanna, was now at her dad's alma mater, Auburn, while her little brother, Chris, was in high school distinguishing himself to such an extent that he would be the valedictorian of his graduating class and win an appointment to the Naval Academy.

In my family, Ralph had graduated with distinction from the University of Florida and had followed me to FSU Law; he started there in the fall of '73, the semester after I graduated. My dad, bursting with pride that both his sons would be lawyers, was still working for the Florida Department of Agriculture, while my mother had a large clientele of customers for her hairdressing home business, especially on Saturdays. The two of them had settled into a more comfortable life. They had made good friends in Gainesville, and my dad's cousins the Mesas, who lived down the street, were constant companions. Margarita, an active girl, was all over the neighborhood on her bicycle. She was sociable, smart, and spoiled. On weekend visits Kitty and I always tried to spend time with her. And my grandmother was still down in Miami, with most of her family now resettled around her. Almost my entire extended family on my father's side was now living in freedom, most of them only three or four hours away by car. We would all get together at least a few times a year. On my mother's side only her sister Yolanda, brother-in-law Rinaldo, and their children were in the United States. The rest of her family remained in Cuba.

Kitty and I were delighted when we learned that my immediate family might return to Orlando. We had scarcely resettled there when my dad started to tell me he wanted to leave Gainesville and come back to his first home in America. As a state employee who had now accumulated some seniority, he was eligible to put in to be transferred there. We were all excited when he landed on the waiting list for transfer.

❖   ❖   ❖

AS THE OLD saying has it, into each life some rain must fall. That was the attitude Kitty and I had whenever we encountered obstacles. But rain falling into one's life is one thing; a hurricane is another.

In late 1974, tragedy struck. Margarita contracted a dreadful disease, a rare and horrible neurological disorder called neurofibromatosis. She was all of fourteen. It started subtly, progressed steadily, and accelerated gruesomely. Yet through it all, despite the acute suffering, Margarita never felt sorry for herself, never lashed out and cried, "Why me?"

The rest of us, though, struggled mightily with it. My mother was in denial the whole time and would not accept what was happening. She resolved to save her only daughter through prodigious care and love showered on her during her every waking moment, supplemented with constant vigilance even when Margarita slept. As my sister deteriorated irreversibly, my mom buckled under the strain, falling apart a few times. My dad, as stouthearted as ever, also found himself unable to handle the decline of his daughter. Unlike my mother, he knew what the disease was doing to Margarita. He used to say to me, "Mel, I wish I didn't know so much about medicine now." Because of this he started to shy away from talking to the neurosurgeon and the other specialists.

Kitty and I had to step up for my parents, especially because Ralph couldn't be around as much as he would have liked, since he had to attend to his law school responsibilities in Tallahassee. Kitty did far more than I did. She left her job, took a break from grad school, and moved to Gainesville. She started sleeping in the daytime so she could relieve my mother at the hospital and comfort my sister. Every night at around nine o'clock she would arrive in Margarita's room and stay there until my mom showed up after breakfast in the morning. Kitty chatted away with my sister when Margarita couldn't sleep and did everything from emptying bedpans to washing and setting her hair and helping her put on makeup. For my part, I conferred with the doctors when doing so became too much for my dad. He leaned on me during this impossibly difficult time.

If my parents found it too painful to talk about Margarita's illness, the truth is that neither could I till now. It has always been one of those things that immediately made me choke up, and I could never find enough air in the room to breathe. But I'm going to try to tell Margarita's story, keeping in the forefront of my mind the example of courage and dignity my little sister set. My hope is that reading this will help others whose families, similarly unfortunate, have been stricken with a tragedy this severe.

❖   ❖   ❖

MARGARITA CAME INTO this world on December 6, 1960, the only member of my immediate family to be born under Communism. My father was forty-three and my mother was approaching forty when my sister was born. To my parents, Margarita was a pleasant surprise, but to Ralph and me she came as a bit of a shock, since our mom and dad did not prepare us well for the arrival of a new baby in the family.

My brother and I went to meet our new little sister on a cool December day. My dad drove up to our school right before our midday break, loaded us into the car, and drove us to the hospital. Ralph and I watched our new arrival in our mother's hospital room. There she was, all pink and wrinkly, as she lay swathed in a little pink blanket in a white bassinet. All doubts and confusion instantly vanished as my brother and I fell hopelessly in love with this tiny person who was joining our family. Papi stood behind us, grinning proudly, as Ralph and I laughed and waved and made goo-goo faces at our new sister. The three Martinez men were like latter-day Magi at the arrival of my dad's only daughter and, for Ralph and me, our only sister. It's a moment that sparkles for me in memory.

My mother was ecstatic to finally have a little girl to dress up and fuss over. Her sisters were thrilled too. They often made the trip from Quemado de Güines to Sagua to check on Margarita, coo over her, and take turns changing and feeding her. Amid the ever-darkening political situation in Cuba, Margarita was a beam of light and an inspiration to our whole extended family. I was especially aware that my time with her was precious. The plans to send me abroad in the Peter Pan program were now well along.

Toward the end of Margarita's first year, as I was waiting only for that vital telegram saying when I was to catch my plane from Havana to Miami, I tried to teach her how to walk. I would stand behind her and she would clutch my two index fingers as I cradled her elbows with my hands and she staggered from one chair to the next in the living room, squealing when she reached the destination chair. I was desperately trying to cram in quality time with her, aware that the clock was ticking and the telegram could arrive any minute. One of my efforts landed me in trouble with my mother. I put Margarita on my bicycle, propping her against the handlebars while clutching her with my one arm and steering with the other hand. I then pumped the pedals all the way across Sagua to my grandmother Graciela's house. It was a long ride and my mother nearly killed me when she discovered this. "She's too young and fragile to do that, you foolish boy," she snapped at me. "What were you thinking?"

I looked at her and said, "I was thinking that when she's old enough I won't be around to do it and she won't know who I am or have any memories of me."

My mother's anger vanished as fast as it had flared. She stared at me openmouthed, clearly touched, then quickly recovered and said, "I see. But she's still too tender for that. You mustn't do it again."

I said I wouldn't.

A few days after this incident I was there for Margarita's first birthday. We had a nice family celebration to mark the occasion. Exactly two months later, to the day, I was gone.

❖   ❖   ❖

THE NEXT TIME I laid eyes on my little sister was four years later, when she was standing on the top of the portable staircase rolled up to the doorway of the National Airlines prop plane that brought her to Orlando. Though she was a little shy when we first met on the tarmac, I quickly developed an intimate rapport with this beautiful, lively, talkative five-year-old. We became fast friends, despite the fourteen-year age difference between us. I spoiled her, taught her English, bought her treats, drove her to and from school every day in the '59 Chevy, and generally tried mightily to make up for the time we'd lost. She picked up English at lightning speed. Popular songs on the radio were a big help here. On our car rides we developed a duet. Together we would belt out the tagline from her favorite song on the radio: "Oh, sweet pea, come and dance with me." She *was* my sweet pea.

Ralph drew closer to her too, despite being ten years her senior. Our mother had had the foresight that enabled us to weather the long separation and develop a close relationship with Margarita. Back in Cuba, she had kept alive the memories of Ralph and me by showing Margarita pictures of her two big brothers and telling her stories about us. She also made sure that Margarita included her exiled brothers in her nightly prayers.

When Kitty entered the picture, Margarita felt as if she'd hit the trifecta: besides having her two big brothers back in her life, she had acquired a new big sister. Kitty would fix her hair, help her put outfits together, take her shopping, and pretend, like Ralph and me, to eat the imaginary food and drink the phantom coffee Margarita made in her tiny play kitchen. When she bonded with Kitty's brother, Chris, at our wedding, it was the beginning of a friendship that would grow strong through the difficult years ahead.

❖   ❖   ❖

THE TROUBLE STARTED deceptively and seemed minor at first. In the summer of 1974 Kitty and I invited Margarita to spend a few days with us in Winter Park. That entire visit we had a great time together, including on a fun-filled excursion to the beach that Margarita loved. By this time, at thirteen, she was developing a healthy interest in boys and she reveled in girl talk with Kitty, who served as a wise and knowing consultant. But when we drove Margarita back down to Gainesville we told my parents that we thought she had a hearing problem and that it should be checked. Kitty and I also commented to each other that she had that teenage clumsiness and was always bumping into furniture and doorways. But we didn't dwell too much on this.

Months later, a few days before Christmas, I was at the office on a Saturday morning when Kitty phoned and said to call my parents; there was a problem. Margarita had been admitted to the hospital. What had appeared at first to be simply a bad case of flu had been diagnosed as a possible brain tumor.

Kitty and I rushed to Gainesville, while Ralph hurried there from Tallahassee. We convened at the Shands teaching hospital at the University of Florida. It was almost immediately apparent to us that this was deadly serious. My parents were trying to cope, but were actually coming apart. One minute Margarita had been a healthy and vibrant teenager with her whole life in front of her. The next minute she was the victim of an awful and agonizing disease that imperiled any future she might have, near or far. The festive Christmas season contrasted starkly with the grim prognosis we had just been handed. It didn't compute.

The whole family soon met with the neurosurgeon, Francisco Garcia-Bengochea. Dr. Garcia was at the top of his field. He was also a Cuban-American who could speak perfect Spanish and communicate in detail with my parents. As sensitive and caring as Dr. Garcia was, there was no way he could sugarcoat what had befallen Margarita: she had not just a tumor but also an especially virulent case of neurofibromatosis. The prognosis was ghastly. It was on hearing this news that my dad bewailed his extensive knowledge of medicine.

I absorbed the brunt of this information as calmly as I could. My father drifted a few paces away, far enough to be out of earshot, while my mother returned to Margarita's bedside the instant she got the gist of what the doctor was saying and then simply ignored it entirely. Dr. Garcia was a great person, full of faith and compassion, and he quickly discerned my father's distress and my mother's denial. Thereafter he would take the time to discuss medical matters with the other members of our family. Because Ralph was then in the midst of law school finals and Kitty was spending all her time caring for Margarita and supporting my mother, the task of dealing with the doctors fell largely on me.

Thrust into this position, I tried to learn as much as possible about my sister's disease. I quickly discovered that a source of innocent amusement for Margarita and me when she was a toddler was actually a bad omen.

Before my exile from Cuba, I used to help my mother bathe her. When I noticed a cute little brown spot on the side of her belly I made a game of it. I used to rub the washcloth on it and say to her, in a falsely scolding voice, "You are dirty here." I would pretend to scrub it clean but actually I would tickle her there until she squealed and giggled with joy, splashing the bathwater with her flattened palms, getting me wet and making me laugh too. But when I researched neurofibromatosis, I learned that such café-au-lait spots were a key diagnostic sign, a telltale indicator of big trouble in the offing for Margarita. This disease was going to ravage her.

❖   ❖   ❖

THE RECOVERY PERIOD from significant brain surgery is long. That holiday season of '74–'75 Margarita spent forty days in the hospital, all through Christmas, New Year's, and beyond. Our extended family rallied to her side, as did the entire Cuban-American community in Gainesville. Visitors were always there, and all visits to the hospital were conducted "Cuban style": the contingents were large, the voices loud, the flowers and get-well cards plentiful. Most of the time the visitors spilled out of Margarita's room and congregated in the corridor outside and even overflowed down the hall into the visitors' lounge. Prayers were offered for Margarita at all the

Spanish masses at St. James in Orlando and in Gainesville at my parents' parish, St. Patrick's. We never lacked for love and support throughout this forty-day ordeal.

But as always is the case, the immediate family had to cope with the crucial issues. Ralph, of course, had to return to law school. He would visit on the weekends whenever he could, studying at our parents' house when he wasn't visiting Margarita in the hospital. I had to return to Orlando to work. But Kitty stayed put, coming through so fervently for my sister—and for my mother—that she became, then and forevermore, a vital part of the family. She was a constant during those forty days, showing up at Margarita's hospital room every night. Margarita loved Kitty and was comfortable with her and, when my sister regained her ability to speak after the operation, she and Kitty chatted large chunks of the night away, often engaging in boyfriend talk, since Margarita never for a moment considered that her illness would curtail her enjoyment of life. She eagerly made plans for her future as though nothing serious had happened.

Her ordeal wouldn't let up, though. My sister would suffer through seven years and four brain surgeries, and all of us Martinezes would suffer along with her. When a catastrophe of this magnitude strikes a family, time seems to stand still. But that's only an emotional and perceptual illusion, because, relentlessly, time marches on and life keeps happening.

❖ ❖ ❖

THE BICENTENNIAL YEAR of 1976 was a time of celebration for the country, and while Margarita's struggles were always with us, the year did bring a few nice developments for the Martinezes. My dad's transfer came through from the Department of Agriculture, and my parents rejoined us in Orlando at last. Kitty and I helped them find a home that was bigger and nicer than either the old Orlando place on Pine Street or the Gainesville house. The new house was situated on a lovely little cul-de-sac and, not insignificantly, had an enclosed garage instead of merely a carport. Like many immigrants before them, they had moved up.

My parents preferred Orlando, and not simply because it brought our family closer together. Being back there also reunited my parents with the city's large Cuban-American community, in which they had many friends. And in general, Orlando offered more than Gainesville, which, though beautiful, was essentially just a big college town. Orlando was starting to boom, as quite a few businesses were setting up headquarters, branches, factories, and plants there. Disney, of course, was the key to the boom, as Orlando catapulted to the top of the list among the world's favorite destinations. The airport became a huge international facility instead of the single terminal my parents had landed at a decade earlier, and hotels sprouted around town like wildflowers in an especially verdant spring.

In June, Ralph graduated from FSU Law School and he, too, came to Orlando. He had secured a job with a good local firm right out of school. He lived with Kitty and me for three months while he boned up for the state bar exam. Once he passed, he promptly got his own apartment in Orlando.

Matters were progressing for Kitty and me as well. The same year my parents and Ralph came back to Orlando, we moved into a new home as well. We were able to sell our starter house at a nice profit and use the money as a down payment on a new, bigger place. It would be our home for the next quarter century. We were moving up too. In fact, I had been made a partner at my law firm, three years after I had started there as an associate.

My law career may have been booming, but Kitty's and my

quest to have a baby was a bust. We had been trying to start a family for some time and were not succeeding. At first we weren't too concerned. Getting pregnant can take time. But by 1976, after six years of marriage, we were feeling frustrated. We had begun to consult doctors about our lack of luck in getting pregnant. The specialists had pronounced everything normal, and yet Kitty still had not conceived. Without an explanation for our childless state, we were starting to despair.

On our sixth wedding anniversary we went out for a romantic dinner and arrived at a momentous decision: we would adopt. I had broached the possibility about a year earlier, but Kitty, naturally, had been determined to get pregnant and give birth to a child. By now, however, she had become reconciled to the idea. The man who had hired me at my firm, Butch Wooten, had adopted his first child, and Kitty and I had often babysat for the Wootens.

Over our candlelit dinner, we decided to contact Tom Aglio, the very same man from Catholic Charities who had helped us Peter Pan kids at Camp St. John in Jacksonville all those years earlier. Tom was now heading up the Catholic Charities office in Orlando. He had, in fact, founded this office at the same time we "Twelve Apostles" from Camp St. John arrived in Orlando to live with our foster parents, with whom Tom had placed us. For years after that, until we reached the age of nineteen and set out on our own, he had monitored our welfare. I was very fond of him, and had kept in contact with him over the years.

Kitty and I thought of Tom because he had set up an adoption agency affiliated with his Catholic Charities operation in Orlando. When I called him he instantly offered to help. Kitty and I went through the normal series of interviews during the screening period. Our home was inspected to ensure it was an appropriate setting for bringing up a child, and we were evaluated to determine how sturdy our marriage was and to plumb our feelings about child rearing. We filled out reams of paperwork and took training classes with six or seven other hopeful couples at the Catholic Charities center. When all of these application and orientation protocols were completed we settled in to wait for a child to adopt. The waiting time was indeterminate but usually took about a year. If you were lucky, it could be much shorter. We rashly presumed we'd be lucky.

On the eve of one full year of waiting, Kitty had a crisis. She so wanted a child that frustration overwhelmed her. On the night of June 12, 1977, a day before our seventh wedding anniversary, she climbed into bed, curled into a ball, and started crying, saying, "I don't understand, I just don't understand. It's a year now and no baby. We have friends who don't want to be pregnant—they're just too busy. Here we are, all we want is to be parents. I simply don't understand what's taking so long. I don't understand why we don't have a baby." I consoled her and held her and told her everything would be all right. We had a tender moment followed by some whispered conversation before she eventually drifted off to sleep, still a little teary, as I held her.

The next morning at seven o'clock, Kitty and I were in the kitchen having breakfast when the phone rang. It was the adoption agency. Our daughter, Lauren, had been born on May 26 and would be ready to be adopted in a week. We were ecstatic, but I pushed the Catholic Charities agency to make Lauren available sooner: the upcoming Sunday was Father's Day. At first the adoption agents resisted, but then, suddenly, they relented.

Lauren was coming in just three days! Ring all the church bells in town!

As soon as we hung up the phone, Kitty and I looked at each

other. We were, of course, overjoyed and awed by this wonderful news. But I could also see contrition and a smidgen of self-rebuke on Kitty's face.

"Do you realize," she said, "when I was crying and in a funk, this decision had already been made? No important decision like this was made at this early hour of the morning. I was in utter despair, and our first child was already on the way."

❖   ❖   ❖

IN THE MONTHS that we waited for Lauren, Kitty was as stalwart and sensible as ever and would not let her imagination run away with her, lest she jinx us. To be sure, when we had gone Christmas shopping at the end of 1976 we had roamed through the children's departments and the toy departments with a gleam of excitement in our eyes as we looked over all the clothes and toys we planned to buy in the not-too-distant future. But we did not make the customary in-home preparations—we didn't paint the nursery, stock it with stuffed animals and dolls, buy baby clothes or furniture, or anything of the sort. Polly had given Kitty the crib that she and Deanna and Chris had slept in, but that was it. As a result, the three days between that joyous early-morning phone call from the adoption agency and the Friday when we brought Lauren home with us were a mad rush of activity. Our friends the Wootens had a shower for Kitty, and the rest of the time she went shopping and got everything for the new baby we'd need, while I painted our daughter's room.

Finally the pickup day came. That was one great Friday for us. Soon after we drove Lauren home, a van pulled into our driveway. It carried everyone from my office except a skeleton crew left behind to man the phones. A small impromptu party broke out, and Kitty and I were beaming. No sooner did this contingent of colleagues leave than the Martinez clan started pouring in, spearheaded by my parents and Margarita. A little later, after work, Ralph showed up too. Aunts and uncles and cousins arrived in a steady stream. Of course this gathering turned into a family party. Food was prepared. Champagne was broken out and corks popped. It will always stand out for me as one of the great days of my life, the day I became a father for the first time, the day my darling daughter enriched our lives, the day the next generation of the Martinez family produced its first member.

Looking at Kitty, I didn't think I had ever seen her happier. I know I had never been happier.

❖ ❖ ❖

MARGARITA, SIXTEEN AT the time, came to our house the day we brought Lauren home. She was wildly enthusiastic about being an aunt for the first time. The disease had not yet ravaged her as it eventually would, and she cradled Lauren in her arms on the sofa in a touchingly proprietary way, not wanting to give her up.

Such happy moments grew increasingly rare for Margarita. She had to undergo three operations following the initial operation. Each time the convalescence was long and painful. She never complained. She insisted on having her social life at the church youth group and managed to graduate with distinction from high school. Unfortunately, her ambitions to attend college were thwarted by her growing incapacities, but she never gave up. After each operation she would emerge with her head swathed in bandages and lose her speaking ability for days on end. Every time she fought hard to regain her speech, although it grew progressively more slurred and harder to understand following each operation.

Not too long after her first niece arrived on the scene, Margarita had to resort to the use of a wheelchair. This is when my good friend from law school Ken Connor came through for us. It so happened that in a case he handled he had met a man whose daughter became a paraplegic as the result of a senseless accident. Back in the 1970s the rights of the physically challenged were not recognized by society as they are today; besides the absence of public facilities to accommodate them, there were no specially equipped vans to transport them so that they would not be rendered totally immobile by their affliction. Realizing this and seizing the initiative, this fellow had bought a van and customized it to accommodate his stricken daughter. Others saw it and wanted one like it. Obviously very able mechanically, this man then went into business customizing ordinary vans to accommodate the physically challenged. Ken in his usual kind way surprised us with one of his used vans. We used the van to take Margarita wherever she had to go, whether it was Dr. Garcia's office, the hospital, school, church, or other family or social functions.

But Margarita's condition continued to deteriorate. My mother, of course, devoted her life to caring for her daughter. As a result, her in-home hairdressing business had ground to a halt, and she could no longer afford time for her English lessons and driving lessons. The worry and frustration that our family shared watching Margarita's heroic struggle cast a pall over all of us, as it does over any family that has had to cope with what is sometimes starkly characterized as a "wasting disease." You watch the loved one fail in stages, and each stage makes a dent in your spirit and takes a chunk of your heart with it.

But as always in the instance of an onslaught of misery, there were countervailing developments. Blessings, really. Ten years after Larry's death, Kitty's mother, Polly, moved to Orlando to be closer to us. By then Deanna had graduated from Auburn and Chris had graduated from Annapolis and started his career as a naval officer. So Polly was there for a truly magical moment: the birth of our first son.

On February 25, 1981, Kitty, after a series of emotionally diffi-cult miscarriages, gave birth to our son John. My father picked up Polly that day and the two of them rushed over to the hospital to see their first grandson. When the two grandparents arrived they were as gleeful as kids on Christmas morning. My father was especially pleased, since he learned that we had given John the middle name of Melquiades. We were passing along a family tradition—the name that had been given to my great-grandfather, my grandfather, my father, and me. Margarita, too, was thrilled to have another baby around, but by now her condition had worsened to the point that it wasn't easy for her to hold John as she had done with Lauren.

One of the final moments of joy for Margarita came on January 8, 1983, when Ralph married a fantastic woman named Becky. I used the specially equipped van to drive Margarita to Delray Beach for the nuptial mass. Despite the toll her disease had taken, she looked radiant in her bridesmaid's dress.

Three weeks later the horrible event happened. With Kitty hold-ing one hand and me the other, Margarita died in her hospital bed at home. My parents, overcome with grief, had retreated to the hallway outside the room.

A day never passes that I do not think of her. Margarita was a wonderful young woman with guts, charm, and beauty. She was just a great person. But she never got to blossom, despite being an inspi-ration to everyone lucky enough to have known her.

AMERICANS: As Kitty and I built our lives
together, we felt privileged to have
our family close by.

Chapter 15

SERVING

THE NEXT PHASE of my life sort of sneaked up and tapped me softly on the shoulder. That I had often dreamed my life would include this next step after practicing law didn't make me any less hesitant to pursue it.

The law had always excited me, and I had succeeded at it far beyond what I had imagined possible. I had even become a name partner at my law firm, which was now called Wooten, Honeywell, Kest & Martinez. My time at Wooten was always enriching, and I had made close friends there, especially with Butch Wooten, who had recruited me to the firm, and Bill Frederick, the senior man at the firm when I started.

Despite all that, after thirteen years at the firm I wanted to strike out on my own. It was the entrepreneurial spirit working in me, inherited, I believe, from my grandfather Melquiades and my dad. Of course I was reluctant to leave my partners, who had been so good to me and to my family, but the idea of creating something from the ground up was too enticing.

Fortunately, I had a great partner in this endeavor: my old friend

Ken Connor. Ever since our days at FSU, Ken had been a constructive influence in my life. He had helped guide me through times when I felt tentative, and his strong faith as a born-again Christian always inspired me. In 1986 the two of us established the law firm of Connor & Martinez.

My office was in Orlando and Ken set up shop in Tallahassee. To our delight, our firm boomed along. But after two and a half years we realized that the two-city arrangement had more complications than benefits, and Ken and I decided to dissolve our partnership, though not our friendship. I then joined forces with Skip Dalton, who had become a friend through the practice and whom I greatly respected as a trial lawyer. We began to practice together in Orlando in what would become Martinez & Dalton.

So I was doing well professionally and personally, not planning to make a major move, when I got a call from Ken Connor in the summer of 1994. Kitty and I were on vacation in the mountains of North Carolina, and I wasn't expecting to hear from Ken. I certainly wasn't expecting what he had to say: he wanted me to be on his ticket as he ran for governor of Florida. So I would be running for lieutenant governor—a position my political mentor Tom Adams had held.

Ken's proposal took me by surprise. It's not that I was unaware of his campaign. He had started it some months earlier, and he and I had talked about it. But I hadn't been expecting him to ask me to join him. I suppose what Ken liked about me, aside from the fact that we had such a strong personal bond, was that I had become an active member of the community. While Kitty and I raised our family we had increasingly been volunteers. I did work for Catholic Charities and served on the school board of Bishop Moore High School, for example. When my law partner Bill Frederick ran for mayor of Orlando I got involved in his campaign, and when he was elected I became part of his inner circle. During his first year he appointed me to serve on the Orlando Housing Authority. I was the first Hispanic on this board; it would be the first of several times that I would break ground as a Hispanic. I also served on the Orlando Utilities Commission. So over the years I had become more and more politically involved.

Still, I hesitated when Ken asked me to run for office with him. I had no doubts about Ken; I believed in his campaign and felt he was running effectively in a crowded field. I just doubted whether running for political office was the right thing for me then. For one thing, Kitty had told me as far back as when I worked for Tom Adams that she wanted no part of a politician's life, with the invasions of privacy and attacks on your character that came with it. Kitty always came first with me (and still does), so naturally I would make no decision without her enthusiastic consent.

I was also hesitant because we had had a fantastic new development in our family. I sometimes think of Divine Providence as a big pendulum. Whenever it swings too far over in one direction, it usually swings back in the opposite direction. So when it swung hard into despondency after we lost Margarita, my faith told me it would rebound. It did. The previous spring the divine spark of life had interjected itself again into our marriage, and nine months later, on September 11, 1993, Kitty gave birth to our irrepressible younger son, Andrew. As the parent of an infant not yet a year old, I didn't know if it would be a good idea to get involved with a political campaign. Kitty and Andrew might need me more than Ken or the State of Florida did.

Had I been at work when Ken called, I would have dismissed his proposal out of hand. But since we were on vacation, I had time to reflect on it and to talk with Kitty about it at length. I knew she shared my great respect for Ken, but she surprised me when she responded favorably to the idea of my joining his ticket. She pointed out how friendly to everyone I had been in school in Tallahassee, both as an undergraduate and in law school. "You never classified people, Mel," she said. "You spoke to the BMOCs and to the shy and retiring guys, the nerds, with the same enthusiasm and warmth. More than one person back then told me you should run for office. I think if you pass this up you'll always wonder how far you could have gone, just like with baseball."

That made me smile. I reminded her that she had told me at FSU that if I planned a life in politics I would need another wife. She laughed and said she had changed. Back then she had assumed that family life was negated and canceled—blighted, really—by a life in politics. But since then she'd seen couples who had maintained close and loving family relationships and still had managed to serve in public office with total commitment to the community. She pointed out that all my commitments in the community had not kept me from the responsibilities as a husband and a father that were so important to me. I still attended the children's school plays and sporting events. I had even been John's Little League coach.

Kitty and I also discussed how our family was at a good point. Yes, Andrew was just a baby, but Lauren was poised to begin her final year in high school and John was about to begin his middle year in junior high school. So our two older children were at an age where they could handle the added stress of politics.

Once I knew Kitty would support me if I made the leap into politics, I took Ken's offer under serious consideration. And Ken did his best to vanquish my doubts. He reminded me how avidly we had studied government and history all during our undergraduate years, and he emphasized how proud Dr. Oglesby, our mentor on those subjects, would be if he could see us enter politics together. Ken said that Professor Oglesby clearly taught us so much about good government in the hope that someday we would put our knowledge to practical use. I also thought of how Tom Adams had quietly urged me toward public leadership.

My main counselor in life had always been my father. This time, however, he was just not well enough to advise me. He had suffered a stroke a couple of years earlier and his health had declined since then. His movements were slow, he tired easily, and his mental sharpness was gone. So I had to draw on the life lessons he had shared with me long ago and that I had internalized. I knew my father had developed a deep suspicion of politics, since even in pre-Castro Cuba the system was corrupt. But I also knew that he believed in giving back to the community that had done so much for our families.

When I thought about Ken's proposal at length, I really did feel that he and I could make a difference in the things we deeply cared about: we could stand up for our beliefs and use our courtroom skills to sell them in the marketplace of ideas. In the end, I remembered my dad's strong convictions about Cuban politics and his admonition that good people didn't go into politics there because the system was so corrupt. I realized that even though my father's hard experience had made him suspicious of politics, he would have been proud of my motivation. I felt that true democracy in America had to be nurtured by good people who entered politics to make a positive difference in life for everyone. If U.S. politics fell to the same sorry state as Cuba and good people stayed out altogether, our democracy could not endure.

I called Ken and told him I was in.

❖   ❖   ❖

IN THE ELECTION we lost badly, but the experience of running for elective office was magnificent. My retail sales experience came in handy on the campaign trail. Just as I had liked helping people by selling them good clothes and shoes, I liked helping them by selling them my vision, my values, and my leadership skills. It was also a lot like persuading jurors in the courtroom, making a point with regular people. I would meet countless people in malls and churches and school halls and town halls and I would get to exchange thoughts and ideas about what we could do to make life in Florida better. We would discuss our conception of what we should do to enhance the chances for our children to succeed in life. Ken and I had a solid vision of what we wanted to bring to government in Florida, but what we didn't have was the money and organization and the network to make that vision possible by getting ourselves elected.

All our flaws were magnified by what our successful opponent did. He was Jeb Bush, and the political organization he had put together was the best—experienced, professional, and committed. This team helped him win that Republican nomination, and from running against him I learned what it would take to win election to public office. Jeb would go on to lose against the incumbent governor, Lawton Chiles, but he would be successful four years later, in 1998.

What was so enlightening and so fortunate for me was that after Jeb defeated us in the primary, we got to know each other fairly well and, as a fellow Republican, I became involved in his campaign in the general election. To say I learned a lot is a total understatement. What's more, I met many people who would prove instructive and helpful to me in years to come. I have spoken to professional boxers who have told me how, when they were just starting out, they were overmatched against a more seasoned fighter who "took them to school." That is exactly what happened to me in my first foray into politics. But by quickly swallowing my pride I undertook an intense seminar in how to do things right in politics. I had done the same as a trial lawyer: when I lost in court I would replay the trial in my mind, not to wallow in defeat but to extract from the loss all that I could apply to ensure future victory.

Throughout this first run for elective office I also learned that the political life could blend successfully with our family life. To my delight, the children took to the campaign enthusiastically and participated with me where appropriate.

So though Ken and I lost in this primary, we won in an important sense. We gained priceless experience. And I learned something vital about myself: I enjoyed the process of running for elective office and felt that I was good at it. I am relentlessly optimistic, especially when it comes to people. Most people are good, kind-hearted, and likable. If you take a quick glance at what people have done for me in my life, my position is easy to understand.

Yet I also fully realize that in public life you can't please everyone. You do your best to get people to buy into your vision and vote for you, but with certain people you will never succeed because you stand for something and have convictions on which you will not compromise. Losing their votes is the price you pay for these convictions.

Having been defeated in my first run for public office, I went back to practicing law. I was not actively planning another run for office, yet I remained open to the possibility, if the appropriate opportunity presented itself.

❖   ❖   ❖

BEFORE THAT OPPORTUNITY arrived I had to cope with another loss in the family. My father had never regained his full powers after his stroke. In fact, his decline accelerated. As everyone knows who has had a loved one felled by a stroke, the first stroke is inevitably followed by others. How long anyone can survive is only a question of how severe and debilitating the strokes are and how durably the victim can withstand them. They always take a toll. With my dad it quickly got bad. The last two and a half years were difficult for all of us.

What made it more painful was that my dad, after so many years of hard work, had finally begun to enjoy retirement. He had worked with the Florida Department of Agriculture until 1988, when he was seventy-one. Even then, he had fought Ralph and me when we tried to persuade him that he should give up the long hours and long drives between food-processing plants and instead spend more time relaxing with family and friends. Eventually he agreed, reluctantly. But he had really taken to retirement. Just as he had gone every day to the café in Sagua, in Orlando he would go to Medina's grocery store, where all the Cuban-American men congregated, and socialize with his buddies over Cuban coffees. He also reveled in taking frequent trips to the Florida Keys to fish with his cousin. Fishing the reefs for yellowtail snapper, Cuban style, with hand lines, reminded him of life in the old country too.

This kind of fun came to an abrupt end about four years into his retirement, when he suffered his stroke. To help him and my mom, I found them a nicer house a few blocks from where Ralph and I lived. It was in a quiet residential neighborhood near Lake Lancaster, only a short drive from downtown Orlando. Just two weeks after Ralph and I settled Mom and Dad into this lovely house, Dad died in the master bedroom. It was August 12, 1995—my parents' fifty-first wedding anniversary. A year earlier we had held a quiet family celebration to mark their golden wedding anniversary, but even then my father's health had deteriorated to such a degree that he was not fully able to enjoy the occasion. A few days after he died, following a mass at St. James Cathedral, we buried him in Orlando in a family plot Ralph and I had bought in Greenwood Cemetery after Margarita died.

Losing my father was extremely difficult for me, as watching his slow decline had been too. It had been painful to have to take his driving privileges away as his health worsened. Now he was gone, and it left a void in my life. He had been not only a dad but also my best friend. I would talk with him about everything. He and I had almost daily telephone chats. He loved to drop by the law firm on his way to some errand. Often we would meet for lunch at a local Cuban restaurant. We went on hunting and fishing trips as long as his health held up. And I always leaned on him for his wise counsel. He took great pride in the fact that I would never buy a car without consulting with him first.

To this day I miss my father. So often when I see a good baseball game on television I want to call and tell him to turn on the game; when I see a beautiful boat on the water I want to describe it to him. I am only comforted by the fact that I have developed a close relationship with my own sons, John and Andrew—as another generation of Martinez men bond with the one above it.

❖ ❖ ❖

TWO YEARS AFTER my father's death, in 1997, I began to hear from friends that I should consider running for the office of Orange County chairman. Orange County's charter had been changed, and the Orange County chairman position was a new one, encompassing the whole county. So it was now a big job, with the chairman functioning as the chief executive of a large central Florida county with 850,000 residents. It was effectively the mayor's job, and is now called county mayor, in fact. Coincidentally, I had been selected as the attorney for the Orange County Charter Review Commission seven years earlier and had, actually, done the legal work that resulted in the creation of the position of county mayor.

With close friends rallying me to take the plunge, including Ralph and my law partner, Skip Dalton, I found the prospect enticing. The mayor's purview covered the entire area that had taken me in when I was a fifteen-year-old exile separated from his family, so on a personal level the job would be my chance to reciprocate to the people who had done so much for me. By then I had lived in central Florida for thirty-six years and had benefited greatly from the community I called home, and I felt that making it a better place was an obligation and a responsibility.

But I don't make impulsive decisions, and I knew there were other considerations to be addressed. Foremost among them was the impact that running for mayor would have on my family. I approached Kitty and the kids about the decision. I wanted to be sure that we were financially secure, and after analyzing the situation, I felt that we were. They agreed. It was also a settled time for us, they felt. The turmoil and grief of losing Margarita and Papi were behind us. Lauren was in college, John was in high school, and Andrew had settled nicely into preschool.

Kitty had always made it possible for me to focus on my professional life, because our relationship was strong and she handled the home front magnificently in addition to her many volunteer jobs. She assured me she could continue to do so if I campaigned and won public office. Kitty and the kids also assured me that I had been a devoted husband and an attentive father, and that this new challenge would not change that.

Still, I wanted to be absolutely certain that the family all agreed that we should throw our hats into the ring and embark on a public life together. So we sat down for a final and formal family meeting.

When they agreed unanimously, any and all doubts about giving this a shot were removed. It was a go.

❖   ❖   ❖

AS SOON AS we decided that I would run, I was determined to succeed. I reduced my workload with the law practice and campaigned almost full-time. I established my campaign headquarters and staffed it fully. I hired political consultants, my good friends John Sowinski and Tré Evers. I enlisted a team of volunteers, including many family members and old friends. I got on the stump. I appeared everywhere I could. I spoke at every kind of gathering, large or small, near or far. I knew the outlying areas of the county from having lived and worked there for so many years.

I ran into people who said they remembered me from years before when I had sold them men's furnishings or shoes at Rutland's. Younger people claimed to know me from my counselor days at Camp Wewa. Still others recalled playing ball against me when I was on the Bishop Moore Hornets or the American Legion Post 242 team. The most touching experience came when I went to a barbecue in rural East Orange County. I was unsure how I would be received there, a downtown lawyer meeting a group of people involved in agriculture. To my great delight I was greeted like a long-lost cousin. Some of these men had known my father when he worked for the Department of Agriculture. I know my dad was smiling from above.

I got a real charge out of meeting so many people, sharing their memories, hearing their problems, listening to their aspirations. It was exciting for me; it drew forth my energy, and it increased my determination to win and thereby improve matters. I wanted to render great service, improve every county resident's quality of life, and help out in any way I could.

When it came to the practical side of running for office, I was fortunate to have the input of my good friend Bill Frederick, who shared what he had learned in his experience as mayor of the City of Orlando. When he was mayor, Bill had been a Democrat, but since then he had converted to being a Republican. He gave me good advice on how to run my campaign, on ensuring that my platform was clear and well developed, and on the key issues facing Orange County. That advice helped me compete in a crowded five-candidate primary and then the final, two-man runoff.

I found myself up against a talented man who had amassed a considerable personal fortune, a large portion of which he was eager to spend in pursuit of victory. Here is where a crucial lesson I had learned in losing to Jeb Bush paid off. I had raised a lot of money, but from Day One my opponent matched it, so I was going to be out-spent. But I was not going to be outworked. There was too much at stake in this election for me to let that happen. We were among the fastest-growing counties in the country. This growth was weighing heavily on the infrastructure we had in place, and it was crowding the schools and straining systems such as our waterworks and our waste and sewage removal. The mushrooming population was stretching the police and firefighting departments to their limits, and our transportation system was now badly in need of updating and expansion. The challenge of rational and prudent development was therefore crucial. The crux of the matter was not only how much we grew but also how we could ensure as we grew that our quality of life remained high.

The valuable advice I received and the hard work our campaign put in paid off on election night. The pundits had forecast a tight race, but on November 3, 1998, I won by a healthy majority, captur-ing 60 percent of the vote and winning in every demographic cate-gory, among every group and type of person in the county.

That night was electrifying. My entire extended family was there for my victory celebration. My mother was overwhelmed and my mother-in-law, Polly, just glowed. The Miami branch of the Martinez family was in attendance. My grandmother Graciela and great-uncle Mariano had since passed on, but Aunt Luisa, who had facilitated my meeting the Peter Pan people in Havana, and who had later taken care of Ralph during his first years in this country, beamed during the whole victory celebration. So did Uncle Eduardo, who had driven me to the airport in Havana the day I left Cuba. The same with my aunt Yolanda and my many cousins; they were just elated.

Their faces radiated joy and pride. As we all know, there are limitless ways to make it in America, but for us Martinezes this was a unique and extraordinary validation that we had indeed arrived. I only wished that my dad and my sister had lived to see it.

❖   ❖   ❖

THE DAY I took office as Orange County mayor was truly special. It marked the culmination of a journey in my home community that had begun at the Greyhound bus station nearly four decades earlier. That's why I wanted my swearing-in ceremony to be a celebration of more than just the taking of an oath.

On the nights before the primary and the general election I had held prayer services at St. James Cathedral. Their purpose was to come together with friends and pray for our community. In the days leading up to both the primaries and the general election I had also visited most of the African-American churches in the county to emphasize that mine would be an inclusive administration. Sunday after Sunday, throughout the campaign, Kitty and I were greatly enriched by the experience of taking in new forms of worship in our community. We had visited Jewish temples, Protestant churches of every persuasion, and, of course, as many Catholic churches as we could. That's why I thought that it would be fitting to hold a communal prayer service at St. James the morning of the day I took office. It was uplifting and inspiring. We then paraded to the county courthouse for the ceremony. I was thrilled to have my family with me: my mother as well as my "other" parents, Mr. and Mrs. Young (Tío and Tía) and June Berkmeyer; Polly; Ralph, Becky, and their children; and, of course, Kitty and our children.

In my speech that morning, I tearfully thanked the Youngs, June Berkmeyer, and my own family for helping me attain this position. I then challenged our community and the county commissioners to fulfill the agenda I had laid out in my campaign, which called for detailed actions to be taken in ten key areas where the quality of life in the community could be significantly enhanced. The words I have so often repeated since then, and which have become a signature statement for me, were first articulated that day as my main "takeaway." I said, "I am a testament to the fact that in America if you work hard, play by the rules, and have an abiding faith in God, all things are possible."

I had crafted a full agenda during my campaign, and I'm proud to report that I followed through on it after I was elected. This book is not about public policy, but I will say that my life experiences had an impact on my agenda and shaped a lot of the actions I took in leading the community. Education was the cornerstone I had built my dreams on, so, when I was mayor, it was always of the utmost importance to me. A compliment I still treasure came when the superintendent of schools characterized me as "a great teacher." I would frequently visit the schools and exhort the students to give their all and never give in. I didn't hesitate to talk about the frustrations I had faced as someone who came to this country not knowing the language or to explain what a huge difference getting an education had made in my life.

I insisted that every child be granted the educational opportunities that had made my incredible life in America possible. That's why I was adamant that no new development could be approved until schools were available. There would be no overcrowding at the expense of even one student's education. This policy has been widely adopted in Florida, I'm gratified to say. In fact, stopping development until schools are available is known throughout the state as the "Martinez Doctrine."

In the same way, my experience doing youth work with the YMCA led me to implement an idea first proposed by my predecessor. I created after-school programs in all of the county's middle schools. These programs were not just done as government initiatives but were carried out in partnerships with the YMCA and with the Boys and Girls Clubs.

Another policy I put into place had biographical overtones too. The issue of health care had touched my life. During my days as a foster child I had relied on the charity of care providers. Hector Méndez, also a Cuban immigrant, took care of all of us Peter Pan children in Orlando for free. During my time as county mayor, 17 percent of the population of Orange County had no medical insurance. In response I started a series of community clinics to care for the uninsured. Again, this program was done as a government partnership with the private sector and with the not-for-profit sector of the community.

My agenda as mayor was always active and busy, and I'm thankful that I was able to actualize the changes I had promised in my campaign. It was wonderfully satisfying to give back to the home community that had been so generous and welcoming to me as a child, then as a student who received a good education, and finally as a lawyer, parent, and community leader.

For two years I worked incredibly hard as Orange County mayor to effect the changes I had promised. Then lightning struck in the form of yet another incredible opportunity.

President Bush tapped me for his Cabinet.

An extraordinary day: Being sworn in as a
U.S. senator was a joyous moment I was blessed
to share with my family. *From left to right:*
My son-in-law, Tim; my daughter, Lauren; my
mother; me; Kitty; Vice President Dick Cheney;
my son John; my son Andrew; Ralph.

Chapter 16

WASHINGTON

THE SAME YEAR I was elected Orange County mayor, Jeb Bush won the Florida governorship. In fact, we had bumped into each other on the campaign trail and he had been very encouraging of my candidacy. So when his brother George, then governor of Texas, came through Orange County on his presidential campaign in 2000, I was delighted to meet him and lend him my support. We spent an entire day together in Orlando and had an instant rapport.

During the course of our chats he mentioned a few things to me that in retrospect I realize were feelers to see if I had any interest in serving in Washington. At one point he told me that when elected he would need good people to come to Washington and help him run the government. (Yes, he was that confident he would be elected, which I liked him for.) I wasn't sure whether he meant he wanted me to help him recruit these people or actually to be one of them. A few more remarks from him in that vein half convinced me there was a good possibility he wanted me to come to D.C. and work with him. Still, in none of my answers was I even slightly presumptuous.

After the presidential candidate left Orlando I went back to my normal business and didn't dwell on those conversations. Then, one day in early December, when the Bush-versus-Gore recount was still in dramatic contention, I was running an Orange County Commission meeting when the small phone mounted under the dais for emergency calls started ringing. I interrupted the session to pick up the call and heard my administrative assistant, Linda Wright, say, "Mr. Martinez, Governor Bush is calling. He needs to talk to you right away."

I adjourned the meeting for lunch a little early and got on the phone with our governor. Jeb immediately told me that his brother George, apparently President-Elect Bush at this point, wanted to know if I would be interested in serving in his Cabinet as secretary of Housing and Urban Development (HUD). Jeb told me to give him a number where his brother could reach me that night.

Despite the earlier, ambiguous hints, I was caught completely off guard. There had been no preliminary background vetting, which I had assumed would precede a phone call like this. Apparently with the recount drama playing out in the foreground, the president-elect had to do things differently. Those due diligence procedures would have to come later.

When I put down the phone I felt stunned but fascinated. Naturally, I called Kitty immediately. She cautioned me not to get too elated because this was by no means a certainty yet. (She would tell me later that she actually didn't believe the job would come through but didn't want to burst my balloon.) That night no call came in and I thought again how prescient the woman I married really was. The next morning Kitty said that it had been a well-meaning gesture by Jeb but that his brother had probably changed his mind. But a little while later Jeb Bush called again to say the president-elect had not been able to call the previous night because of other urgent business. He asked for a number where I could be reached over the next several days.

A few days later the phone rang and it was Dick Cheney, the (apparent) vice president–elect. Even though the recount was still going on, he told me the Bush team had decided it couldn't wait any longer to start putting the Cabinet together. He asked me to plan a trip to Washington so the two of us could meet and discuss the job at HUD. This was all getting very real.

When I got off the phone, Kitty reminded me that over the past few years she had become open to the idea of relocating somewhere else if I ever got a chance at a sabbatical for a year or so. As she had phrased it to me more than once about such a possibility, "I am there. It would be so much fun." She felt that we had been plodding along devotedly for twenty-five years as I built up my law practice, and that stepping out a bit would not be a bad thing for us to do.

So I arranged to go to Washington to meet with Dick Cheney. In the meantime the U.S. Supreme Court finally broke the deadlock between Bush and Gore, upholding the official certification that George W. Bush was the winner. When I got to D.C., then, it was all official: I was meeting with the vice president–elect of the United States. Still, everything had to stay hush-hush. Nobody could know about these Cabinet maneuverings, and the Bush-Cheney team certainly didn't want word getting out in the press.

I had never met Vice President–Elect Cheney before, and I didn't know what to expect from our meeting. From a distance he seemed more than a little intimidating, but from the minute I walked into his office he was friendly, relaxed, and engaging. We got along just fine. He said, "Well, both Governors Bush speak highly of you. So tell me the basics of your life story." I ran through my background, and when I finished, he said, "That's one terrific story."

The preliminary vetting that I had been expecting earlier now began. By the time I met again with President-Elect Bush in Washington, on December 19, the rumor was flying all over the place that I would be chosen for HUD secretary. It was even being discussed openly in the media. That morning at the transition team's headquarters at the Madison Hotel, I met with the president-elect, Vice President–Elect Cheney, and Andy Card, who would be White House chief of staff. The four of us conversed for thirty or forty minutes. The president-elect was his usual energetic and direct self. He said, "I'm going to get to the point. I want you to be my HUD secretary. Do you want to do it?"

Without hesitation I replied, "Yes."

We began a wide-ranging discussion about the HUD job, as the president-elect assured me that he would have an energetic home ownership agenda. Then he zeroed in on the issue of ethics in a department that had known its share of scandals. He said, "I am told you have a strong ethical backbone and are a good lawyer. That's just what I need at HUD."

Before the conversation ended, I felt it necessary to address an issue of profound importance to my life, one that had been a major motivation for me to enter politics in the first place. I said to him, "Mr. President, during the time I am privileged to serve, I would hope that I could have a voice on issues relating to Cuba. I would like to have an opportunity to play a role in such decisions as are made in this regard."

Andy Card spoke up quickly, stating flatly that foreign policy would fall outside the purview of the secretary of HUD. But President-Elect Bush replied just as quickly, saying without qualification, "Mel will be able to have something to say on Cuba." And that has ever since been the case, and I will forever be grateful to

President Bush for including me in all discussions of his administration's official policy toward Cuba.

At the end of the meeting, the president-elect turned to me and said, "I want you to fly to Austin with me tonight and we'll announce your appointment tomorrow."

Yes, this was real, all right. It was a rush. But I also couldn't imagine this moment without Kitty. "Can my wife join us?" I asked. Of course she could, the president-elect replied.

When the meeting ended, I left the Madison Hotel with a real glow beginning to suffuse me. All that remained was the background check. I sat with Fred Fielding of the transition team, who had been White House counsel for President Ronald Reagan, and answered every question he had. I knew how serious the background check was, for me and for the administration.

Before I knew it I was flying down to Texas that night with the president-elect on his chartered campaign plane (he was not entitled to use Air Force One until he was officially sworn into office). I watched as he worked diligently on his inaugural address with speechwriter Michael Gerson, who was to remain his principal speechwriter for the next several years. Gerson would go on to help write the inspiring speeches President Bush gave after the horrifying events of 9/11. I found it instructive and fascinating to watch how closely the two of them worked on this speech. And yet, despite being totally focused on shaping his speech, the president-elect still found time to look up and chat from time to time with me and Ann Veneman, the designee for secretary of agriculture. I was impressed with his ability to compartmentalize with that much ease and fluidity.

The next morning in Austin I prepared some remarks. I wanted them to be just perfect, and I worked on them as carefully as I had seen the president-elect and Gerson working on the inaugural address. When the time came for the official news conference, President-Elect Bush announced three Cabinet appointments: Don Evans for Commerce, Ann Veneman for Agriculture, and me for HUD. With Kitty looking on I proudly delivered my remarks and felt a splendid rush when I'd completed them. Afterward Kitty and I enjoyed a special moment of serenity and satisfaction with the Bushes and the other appointees, but this tranquil mood would not last long. We were heading back to Orlando that night, and there was much to do.

Not only did we have to complete all the usual preparations for Christmas, which was now just a few days away, but also, Casa Martinez was inundated with congratulatory notes, letters, phone calls, and e-mails. Bouquet after bouquet of flowers arrived at our house. Visitors and well-wishers poured through our front door, overwhelming us. It was bedlam, total bedlam. This was all very flattering, definitely, but it was a bit chaotic. It was especially strenuous for Kitty, the family organizer and executive. On top of everything, she needed to find a house in the D.C. area that the family could move into in a matter of weeks and arrange a new school for Andrew to attend up there. Meanwhile, I had to deal with wrapping up the job of mayor, and as excited I was about the new opportunity I felt some anxiety about leaving the job that I had worked so hard to attain and that I felt so good about doing.

The hubbub eventually died down, and Kitty and I were delighted to find ourselves at the Inaugural Ceremony for President Bush a month later, seated very close to the president. It was a proper introduction to the new world of Cabinet life in Washington. The atmosphere bristled with joy, excitement, and hope. I could not help but marvel at the peaceful transfer of power in the world's greatest democracy. What a contrast it formed to the land of my birth.

❖   ❖   ❖

AS ORANGE COUNTY mayor I had supervised six thousand employees and managed a budget in excess of a billion dollars. HUD had almost twice as many employees and a budget about six times larger. What was daunting was changing the culture of an entrenched bureaucracy. HUD had a reputation for unresponsiveness and a history of some corruption. Some programs had gone far afield from their well-intentioned beginnings and did not serve the public interest. I am proud to say we made inroads on these problems. We tried to change the culture, and in the end, lots of progress was made. I am especially proud that I was able to raise morale while carrying out the president's agenda. I made it a priority to have good relations with the White House and to assist in conveying the president's message to the country: he wanted to increase home ownership, particularly in the Hispanic and the African-American communities, where home ownership lagged behind the national average; to reduce homelessness; to implement the faith-based initiative; and to improve the house-settlement process. On all of these top issues real gains were made.

As it turned out, my time as head of HUD was marked by involvement on international issues as well. The president, as always, kept his word and let me participate in decisions affecting Cuba. In fact, I became a key adviser on Cuban policy. While I was serving in President Bush's Cabinet I was named co-chair, along with Secretary of State Colin Powell, of the Commission for the Assistance to a Free Cuba.

My responsibilities as HUD secretary changed immeasurably and irrevocably a scant eight months into my tenure. That's when the tragedy of 9/11 struck. Suddenly security factors became paramount in our department's plans. I had enjoyed traveling with the president and doing housing events, but these now would rightfully take a backseat for several months. More immediate responsibilities became my focus. HUD was charged with funneling the funds Congress appropriated for the reconstruction of Lower Manhattan. I worked closely with Governor George Pataki and Mayor Rudolph Giuliani during these trying times.

That tragic day of 9/11 and its aftermath are vivid to me, indelibly incised on my memory. We had top-secret emergency briefings on possible follow-up attacks and potential future targets of terrorists. I observed the president in meeting after meeting rising to the occasion and meeting the challenge. We were now a wartime Cabinet, and understandably the focus shifted to national security and away from the domestic agenda.

There were the healing ceremonies at the National Cathedral on the following Friday and the National Day of Prayer. There was a seemingly endless progression of memorial services, because we had lost so many innocent people. The grief of the surviving family members was heartrending, and then there was the wrenching experience of watching those in New York City who could not find a single trace of their lost loved ones.

I will never forget visiting the devastated sites in Manhattan and at the Pentagon. In Lower Manhattan I studied the fences with photos of the missing and poignant pleas and prayers for help. I visited the emergency hubs set up in the schools, churches, and community centers. I rode in an NYPD helicopter over Ground Zero and was sickened to see the total devastation. I watched in stunned awe the mass funerals and burials for the brave police officers and firefighters and observed their widows and orphaned children walking behind their flag-draped caskets in solemn corteges. I visited firehouses that had lost more brave men than had survived.

It was an honor to be able to help out in such tragic circumstances and to bring at least a modicum of comfort to so many people so drastically afflicted.

For all of my adult life I have been a huge fan of Winston Churchill's and I read his writings often and carefully. He knew more than a few things about meeting challenges, handling tragedies, making tough decisions, and inspiring people in dire straits to persevere. Living through 9/11 and its traumatic aftermath gave me an increased appreciation for the qualities of good leadership in trying times, and I hope that I will be able to draw upon what I learned then to help people in extreme circumstances for the rest of my life, whether in an official capacity or simply as another citizen volunteer lending a helpful hand.

❖   ❖   ❖

ASIDE FROM THE honor of serving in the president's Cabinet and the challenge of overseeing a large federal agency, my position as HUD secretary brought me an unexpected benefit: the opportunity to meet dozens of others who had been children of the Peter Pan program.

President Bush often spoke of my history as a Peter Pan. As I traveled around the country, I met many other people who had gone through the same experience. I cherished these encounters, because we Peter Pans share an intense bond that will never be broken.

In an unusual twist of fate, one of those Peter Pans was a fellow appointee of President Bush. A few months after I settled in Washington I met Eduardo Aguirre, whom the president had appointed to the Export-Import Bank. As we chatted I learned that he was a banker from Houston who had come to America as a Peter Pan. One of the first questions Peter Pans always ask one another is, "What day did you leave Cuba?" All of us know the exact date. When I told

Eduardo that I came over on February 6, 1962, he immediately realized that that was the same day his brother Luis had. Eduardo, who had come to America a few months earlier, was at the airport to greet Luis that day. He told me that he clearly remembered a tall thin kid coming down the steps from the same plane his brother was on.

Another question Peter Pans ask when they meet fellow alumni is: "What camp did you go to?" In another odd twist, I realized that Eduardo and his brother were the Aguirre brothers who had been my companions at Camp Matecumbe. President Bush had reunited us in Washington all these years later. Eduardo has served with distinction as U.S. ambassador to Spain in President Bush's second term.

❖   ❖   ❖

MY TIME AT HUD, as rewarding as it was, as educational as it was for me in terms of managing a big government agency, was destined to end when friends and Senate leaders started to urge me three years later to run for the vacant Senate seat in Florida. The chance to become a senator represented a dream come true. And to be completely frank, as much as I enjoyed the Cabinet position, I felt somewhat cut off from my local Florida roots. Then zooming into my life came the opportunity to render more service to my home state, to the welcoming people who had made possible my life in America. I knew instantly I wanted to pursue this new possibility.

President Bush cheerfully accepted my resignation from the Cabinet and told me that he looked forward to talking to me again soon when he would have the pleasure of addressing me as "Senator." As always he was his confident and positive self, never even for one moment entertaining the possibility of my losing the election. He and Laura invited Kitty and me to the White House for a private farewell dinner. It was a tremendous send-off, with each of them giving us lots of valuable campaign advice. We would all four be reunited again on several occasions on the campaign trail as he ran for reelection and I for the Senate.

After a difficult, tightly contested election campaign, fought hard every step of the way, I emerged victorious. I was the new senator from Florida. It was especially enjoyable when the president called to congratulate me on election night and did indeed address me as "Senator Martinez." But it was equally thrilling when former Florida state senator Tom Adams called and used the same term. This was the man who had first inspired my interest in public service so many years before, and who himself so loved to be addressed all his life as "Senator."

MEMORIES OF MY HOMELAND: I have never set
foot in Cuba since I left in 1962. Just as my
father did, I dream that someday
I will walk in a free Cuba.

DREAMS

THE KEENEST PLEASURE I have when out traveling the state to meet people concerned with issues that I must bring before Congress is that in quiet moments they often share their life stories with me. Their stories always give me a keen sense of what drives them, what motivates them, what they care about passionately; this tells me more than a dry explanation of their position on some policy dispute ever could. And when I look back over my *own* story and see it in its entirety, like a single snapshot, I realize that it reveals a lot about my lifelong motivations.

The wrenching experience of exile from my native country and then the immigrant experience have motivated my interest in government and international affairs. But there was another galvanic event that helped propel me into public life. In the mid-1980s I came across a book written by Armando Valladares called *Against All Hope.* This memoir detailed the twenty-two years Valladares spent in Castro's wretched prison system. He was imprisoned for so many years because of his unwillingness to bend to the Communist system; for his resistance he was shuffled from one jail to another, the conditions in each more deplorable and degrading than the last.

Valladares faced torture on an almost daily basis. It was a living hell. The only reason he finally regained his freedom was that he had begun writing poetry that was smuggled out of prison and became known around the world. That spawned an international effort in support of his release. Ultimately the French government intervened, going directly to Fidel Castro to get Valladares out.

Without exaggeration I can say that reading this powerful book changed my life. As I read Valladares's harrowing story I could not help but compare what was happening in his life with the events taking place in my own life at the same time. The contrast was stark. As he would land in some barbaric, oppressive situation, I would say to myself, "That's the year I started at Orlando Junior College." Or, "That was a month after I started law school." Or, "Gosh, Kitty and I were married a month before he suffered that terrible beating." Such thoughts overwhelmed and disturbed me. While all this horrible suffering was being inflicted on a fellow Cuban for having had the temerity to speak out against oppressive conditions under the Castro regime, I was far removed from his suffering and his cause. Certainly I was grateful to have escaped to the comfort and freedom of America, but on a deep level my detachment was unacceptable to me. I resolved to do something about such suffering being inflicted on innocent people in Cuba.

Propitiously, I came into contact with a Cuban-American organization that at the time was dedicated to lobbying Congress to promote freedom and democracy in Cuba. This group had convinced Congress and President Ronald Reagan to allocate funds for broadcasts and telecasts to Cuba. The result was not only Radio Martí, named after José Martí, Cuba's George Washington, but also, years later, TV Martí. Together these two conduits of information have served as a lifeline to the people of Cuba, since the Communist government for years did not allow access to cell phones or the Internet and has controlled the news through the state-run propaganda machinery. These outlets have served the same function for Cuba as Radio Free Europe did for Eastern Europe while it suffered under Communist rule.

I saw these successful results, and my involvement with this organization, and my awareness of its efforts for the cause of a free Cuba, led me to focus on my Cuban heritage in a way I hadn't probably since I was at Camp St. John in Jacksonville. I realized just how important it was to influence the American government in trying to improve conditions for the Cuban people. Every year I would attend a conference in Washington where government officials would update us on America's Cuba agenda and we would walk the halls of Congress to lobby on behalf of a pro-democracy policy for Cuba.

When the Berlin Wall came down and all of Eastern Europe threw off the Soviet shackles, I became convinced that Cuba's day of freedom was near. Sadly, significant change didn't happen in Cuba then, but my interest in America's Cuban policy kept growing steadily with each passing year.

The idea of a career in public office grew even more appealing because I felt it could enable me to make a real difference not just in my community but more broadly, including in the lives of Cubans who were not free to speak for themselves. Little did I know that within a decade I would become one of the principal advisers to the president of the United States on matters relating to Cuba.

❖   ❖   ❖

WHILE I WAS mayor of Orange County one instance of my congressional testimony placed me at the center of an international controversy. I appeared before the Senate Judiciary Committee on

March 1, 2000, to testify on behalf of a young Cuban boy named Elián González. I was so willing and eager to do this because, thirty-eight years earlier, I had essentially been just like him.

The boy had survived crossing from Cuba on a raft that had overturned, drowning his mother and others on board. Miraculously plucked from the sea while clinging for his life to a piece of flotsam from the raft, he had ended up in Miami, where a controversy soon broke out during the long Thanksgiving weekend over whether he needed to be returned to his father in Cuba. The Cuban government launched a public-relations drive designed to elicit international sympathy for the father back in Cuba, who, they contended, had been deprived of his little boy. Like most Cuban-Americans I was convinced that the father was not acting of his own free will in requesting the return of his son. We believed that his father was simply being coerced and exploited for political reasons. We did not want to see this unfortunate youngster used as a political football. Along with several of my Peter Pan friends, I felt that the right thing would be to allow a family court in Florida to decide the boy's fate, based on the *child's* best interest.

Moreover, the stand the Cuban government took did not take into account the well-documented and seemingly endless human rights violations perpetrated by the Castro regime, and it did not factor in that the boy's mother had to be desperate to hazard the ninety-mile crossing of the Straits of Florida on a flimsy, unsafe, makeshift raft to deliver herself and her son to freedom. She had perished along the way but her boy had indeed made it to freedom. His dead mother's dream deserved to be honored. As I and a great many fellow Cuban-Americans saw the situation, her dream of freedom for her son, obtained under near miraculous conditions, was now to be callously renounced for spurious "diplomatic" reasons having to do with not offending the Castro regime.

The perilous sea crossing the mother had undertaken to attain freedom can perhaps only be fully understood from the perspective of a person who has lived under brutal tyranny. My parents had felt that same desperation when they heroically sacrificed their loving proximity to me so that I might live with freedom and safety in the United States. They had made that agonizing decision rather than risk my suffering the same fate that Armando Valladares had endured in Cuba, tortured and languishing in subhuman conditions in filthy prisons. Or, worse, I might well have been stood against a wall before a firing squad, without benefit of a fair trial, and my life instantly snuffed out, as had been the fate of the sixteen-year-old boy named Mirabales from my hometown of Sagua.

I felt an even deeper connection to Elián González because my own son Andrew was exactly the same age as this Cuban boy. As the controversy began to swirl about, I thought it would be nice to at least give Elián a great and memorable day in America, a day any little boy would love to have.

On a quiet day in January 2000, two months after the whole ordeal started, Kitty and I took Elián and Andrew to Disney World. Working with the Disney people, I had arranged to give the Cuban youngster a day at the amusement park free of press and photographers dogging his every footstep. To keep word of this visit from leaking, we had to use a lot of stealth. We had to give the slip to the relentless media horde that trailed the boy wherever he went. We used a special entrance graciously provided by Disney and spent the day sequestered from all media. Disney had one video cameraman unobtrusively recording the proceedings to preserve the memory for Elián. It was a marvelous day. Elián felt at home with me speaking fluent Spanish to him. Seeing the joy on that little boy's face was priceless.

But then something disturbing happened that I will never forget.

Kitty and I took the boys to the ride called "It's a Small World." As we approached the ride, Elián panicked: he saw that he would have to get into a small boat. He had no idea that the water was only about a foot and a half deep, and of course he was having a flashback about his mother's disappearing from that rickety raft and drowning. Scared to death, he refused to get into the boat for the ride. I could see the dread on his face. It was an awful moment in an otherwise glorious day. Only by consoling him and reassuring him that the ride would be safe and fun were we able to pull Elián back from his fear.

A little more than a month later, I was testifying before the Senate Judiciary Committee on Elián's behalf, appearing at the request of Senator Connie Mack of Florida. I was only too happy to do my part. But in the end my testimony was to no avail: the boy was returned to Cuba. This broke my heart. It would have been much easier to accept the outcome had it been the result of a decision by a family court.

Despite the negative outcome of the Elián González story, I will continue to help unfortunate people seeking freedom and dignity whenever and wherever they cross my path. Back in 1980, thousands of Cubans fled en masse for the United States in what became known as the Mariel Boatlift. At the request of Tom Aglio, my old social worker with Catholic Charities, Kitty and I got involved in resettling some of those refugees. That wasn't the first time for us, either. Though I had never made a big point of it, while I was running for Orange County mayor word came out that back in the 1970s I had taken a Vietnamese refugee family under my wing and helped them resettle after they managed to flee the Communists who had swept into power across their entire country. These new immigrants, and many others like them, faced the same trying challenges I faced in 1962 when I landed at Miami International Airport. They needed help, just as I had once needed help. I was determined to provide it, and I would do the same thing again.

One of my proudest moments as a senator came when, working with the president and the secretary of state, I helped obtain the release of Thoung Nguyen "Cuc" Foshee, a Vietnamese-American who had been imprisoned while visiting her native country and held for more than a year. Her crime? She was a strong voice for democracy in her homeland. It is sad to see that the freedom and liberty we so take for granted are not enjoyed by many people in the world.

❖   ❖   ❖

OFTEN IN MY life people have said that I am a self-made man. I always appreciate the compliment, but in truth I don't consider it to be accurate. Rather than being "self-made," I was formed by all the loving people who cared for me and helped me throughout my life. I never doubt that fact.

No one helped make me who I am today more than my father. He was a dauntless crusader for doing the right thing in life, no matter the circumstances and no matter the consequences. His influence on me is incalculable. He had the same effect on my brother, Ralph.

Like me, Ralph can never forget that moment back in Cuba when as boys he and I huddled together on the floor, Ralph's teeth chattering, as gunfire erupted all around us.

I can see my father in Ralph even today—not just in my brother's gestures and expressions, but also in his actions, his unrelenting probity, his unshakable character, and his positive outlook on life. My friends from Bishop Moore High School, Rich Steinke and Gary Preisser, tell me the same thing about myself: that I'm a lot like my dad. This trumps any compliments about being "self-made."

Whenever they say this to me they always laugh and remark about my father, "He was such a character." They mean how genial and people-oriented he was, how outgoing and helpful, how unbendingly decent and honest. He was the quintessential stand-up guy. He personified the idea of people banding together and helping one another in a collective effort. I suppose that's how when I ran successfully for Orange County mayor I came to take as my campaign slogan "Together we can; together we will." The good qualities, the good things about who I am, I think in most ways are because of him.

In fact, when I look back, I see that one crucial turning point in my father's life had an indelible impact on my own life, leading me to who and where I am today.

❖   ❖   ❖

THAT DAY IN 1958 when Ralph and I ended up on the floor of the bedroom, while bullets flew outside, occurred during a failed overthrow of the Batista government. My father had rushed home in the car to get to his family as quickly as possible. On his way home, speeding as fast as he could, he was halted by a single Batista soldier pointing a rifle at him from his post behind a tree, forcing him to slam on the brakes. My dad recognized this soldier as a member of the Batista rural guard who often pulled duty at the local slaughterhouse where my dad had to inspect the animals. The soldier recognized my father just as quickly, so he frantically waved him on, out of the line of fire. My dad was no supporter of the corrupt Batista government, but for the rest of his life he remained convinced that this man had saved his life.

Immediately after the Communists took over in Cuba, their zeal to eliminate all vestiges of the past became very pronounced. The soldiers who had served in Batista's armed forces were immediately detained and tried as war criminals. It didn't matter whether they had done anything inappropriate or not; all that mattered was that they had worn the uniform. Sure enough, the soldier who had spared my dad came under the Communists' system of "lightning justice."

The Castro regime implicated the soldier in the death of a bus driver that had occurred the same day he had allowed my father to pass freely. My father was sought out and asked by the man's defense lawyer to give testimony on the soldier's conduct that day. My dad was being asked to validate the fact that this man was not trigger-happy, was not in fact an indiscriminate murderer, but that he had calmly and reasonably allowed my father to pass unmolested. But around this same time, Castro's regime started to pressure my dad not to testify. These trials were not conducted by adhering to any standard of law or to any code of justice. They were "show trials" done for maximum theatrical effect; in fact, instead of in a courtroom, some trials were held in a local theater. Verdicts were rendered quickly, and death sentences were meted out even faster.

I will never forget watching my father struggle with this momentous—and dangerous—decision. It was obvious to me even then that he had plenty to fear and that it would be better if he somehow avoided testifying. Everyone in my family urged him simply to bow to the government's pressure and not to go. But in the end my father insisted that he would testify and further insisted that he would tell the truth and nothing but the truth, and therefore, he said, he would have nothing to fear.

I have always remembered the valuable lesson he demonstrated in that grim situation. He showed that speaking the truth has a very deep and significant meaning. Standing up for what's right can carry a price, he made clear to me, but no matter the price, standing up for the truth is a moral obligation. As it turned out, my father got lucky and suffered no repercussions for his testimony. The soldier had no such luck: he was found guilty and summarily executed, showing exactly how ruthless the Communist regime was.

Ever since then I have tried to follow my dad's example. In my study at home in Orlando I have mounted on the wall the brass plaque that used to adorn the outside of his veterinarian's office in Sagua. It says, MELQUIADES MARTÍNEZ, MÉDICO VETERINARIO. A relative brought it to me here in America. I treasure having it. It's a constant reminder of him.

Though he is gone, I have continued to dream my father's dream as well. It's a dream shared by millions of Cubans. I dream that someday I will walk with my family beside me, and with my dad's spirit to guide me, in a free Cuba where the people live under a just government and are free to worship as they choose and to live as they desire. America made a great dream come true for me and for my family, and I trust that God will make the enduring dream of a free Cuba, which I still share with my father, come true as well.

ACKNOWLEDGMENTS

W RITING THIS BOOK has been a journey through time and it has opened many emotions. No one knows my story better than my wife, Kitty. Through the years Kitty has patiently listened to many of the stories I have told here. She has been a coach and a mentor as well as an invaluable source of details that I might have overlooked but that were important to my story. She continues to teach me English and has done so here as well. She has freely given of her time to help with this book, and she and our son Andrew have given of our family time to allow me to complete this project.

My agent, Alex Hoyt, made this book possible with his careful guidance and advice. Ed Breslin has become a friend through the writing of the book. Having grown up in two very different worlds, we learned with surprise how much we have in common. He immersed himself in my story and helped me tell it.

My brother, Ralph, is the family historian and was a wonderful resource because he has an excellent memory of events, especially during our youth in Cuba. His wife, Becky, dedicated a lot of time to securing many of the photos.

Linda Wright, who was my legal secretary for twenty-five years, volunteered to type this manuscript. She is a friend and, as always, did a flawless job. My mother-in-law, Polly Tindal, gave me helpful details to fill in some gaps for me. Many of the people who touched my life were also consulted for details and information, among them Cesar Calvet, Rick Steinke, Gary Preisser, Larry Mullan, Tom Aglio, Ken Connor, Jim Corrigan, and Bill VanDercreek.

Finally, I want to thank my editor, Jed Donahue, who understood my story and allowed me to tell it as I wanted, and the rest of the team at Crown Forum, especially Mary Choteborsky, Sibylle Kazeroid, Lenny Henderson, Jie Yang, Melanie DeNardo, Christine Aronson, Donna Passannante, and Shawn Nicholls.

ABOUT THE AUTHORS

MEL MARTINEZ is a U.S. senator from Florida and the former chairman of the Republican National Committee. Born in Cuba, he arrived in the United States at age fifteen. He knew barely a word of English but learned the language, earned his undergraduate and law degrees from Florida State University, and went on to practice law for twenty-five years. Moving into a career of public service, he was elected Orange County (Florida) mayor and then was appointed secretary of Housing and Urban Development in the Cabinet of President George W. Bush. Today, Senator Martinez serves as the first Cuban-American in the U.S. Senate. He lives in Orlando with his wife, Kitty. They have three children.

ED BRESLIN is a writer living in New York City.